T0354780

SPIRITUAL HORS D'OEUVRES

...whet your spirituality...

RONALD W. RAMSON, C.M.

ARCHWAY
PUBLISHING

Archway Publishing books may be ordered through booksellers or by contacting:

Archway Publishing
1663 Liberty Drive
Bloomington, IN 47403
www.archwaypublishing.com
844-669-3957

ISBN: 978-1-6657-4540-6 (sc)
ISBN: 978-1-6657-4541-3 (e)

Library of Congress Control Number: 2023910975

Print information available on the last page.

Archway Publishing rev. date: 7/11/2023

PREFACE

Remember almost half a century ago when now Saint Pope John XXIII opened the second Vatican Council?

He challenged the Church to "Read the signs of the times" so we could respond to the spiritual longings of the people today.

One such "sign of the time" for authors who dare attempt a book to help folks grow in their faith and holiness is the preference for crisp, punchy tips on sanctity.

Father Ronald Ramson, a seasoned (he tells me that's just euphemism for "old") priest of the Congregation of the Mission (Vincentians), has read the signs very well. He detects a longing for spirituality, and a desire for daily, short doses of vitamins for the soul.

That he has succeeded in giving us such a boost of a book is no surprise at all to me. I've known him as a friend and mentor for over four decades. I've watched him in action as a pastor, a missionary in Kenya, a seminary rector, spiritual director, confessor, preacher, author, and retreat director.

When people praise him – as they often do, to his blushing chagrin – they will unfailingly comment, "he's so practical."

So was St. Vincent DePaul; so was Blessed Frederic Ozanam, about whom Father Ramson has written; so was Jesus. The Lord preferred direct, simple, colorful, earthy lessons.

No wonder I found this valuable work so "gospel-like." If you're looking of a cerebral, complicated, erudite theological tome, don't order or buy this book.

If you want some homey, touching, wise daily counsel on how to deepen your faith and enhance your friendship with Jesus, this is your lucky day.

Because that's really what it all comes down to, isn't it? As Pope Benedict XVI exhorted, "I call you to holiness of life, which means friendship with Jesus. I can assure you Father Ron Ramson's closest friend is Jesus. I bet you after reading this book, you'll be closer to the Lord as well.

Faithfully in Christ,
✝ Timothy Michael Cardinal Dolan
Archbishop of New York

NOTE

I wrote this manuscript in Dallas, Texas while I was a spiritual director at Holy Trinity Seminary and revised it in Perryville, Missouri. The material was written ante and post coronavirus pandemic.

One of the things that a good number of us learned during the world-wide viral crisis is the need for personal reflection and prayer. The lock-down provided us with huge chucks of time, time for prolonged periods of pondering on the true priorities of life. Hopefully, for many, the need for reflection and prayer has been developed into a spiritual habit, a new personal treasure.

The following reflections are intended as spiritual hors d'oeuvres to be consumed before your coffee/tea, breakfast, lunch, or dinner.

> *Bless us, O Lord, and these your gifts, which we are about*
> *to receive, from your bounty, through Christ our Lord.*
> *Amen.*

You will discover a good amount of *me* -- autobiographical material -- in the subjects. I sincerely hope that this is helpful and will perhaps recall good memories for you. Enjoy the spiritual hors d'oeuvres!

SUGGESTION

May I suggest a method for you? Pick a subject that fits your fancy. Ponder the subject, pray over it. Make practical resolutions for your life.

Check off a subject each time. Perhaps you will want to review or re-ponder a subject that has spoken to your heart. You will find here over 200 possibilities.

Practice a corporal and spiritual act of charity toward others but don't forget yourself.

INTRODUCTION

I was going to entitle this book *Hors d'oeuvres for Christians* but I was afraid that people would mistake it for a cookbook! Then I thought of *Starters for Reflection* with the subtitle: *Spiritual Hors d'oeuvres*, all with the hope that it might convey what I had in mind. I settled for the latter as the main title because it states my intentions more accurately with the aid of the subtitle.

It is not unusual in a restaurant to see a menu with "Starters" at the top of the first page, or to have a server ask you, "Would you like a starter?" I have heard that question many times in Kenya. In many places of our world, a starter is referred to as a first course of a meal: an appetizer, tapas, meze, antipasto, or hors d'oeuvre. The first and second plates come after, crowned by a luscious dessert.

When I was a kid growing up, I do not remember us having starters or hors d'oeuvres, except for one item. When I saw that particular platter, I knew that, not only was the meal that day going to be special, but the celebration too was intended to be a cut above.

We had an oval-shaped platter (I think it was made from aluminum, not silver). My grandmother, Maude, or my mom, Lucille, would place red raspberry preserves in the center of the tray, probably Smucker's. Then they would ring the jam with Philadelphia Cream Cheese and then the outer ring was Ritz Crackers. I liked the taste of the combined three and still do. That was the only "starter" I remember growing up on North Avenue or West Schubert, in Chicago.

All spiritual hors d'oeuvres in this book are intended to "whet your appetite" -- to kick-start your personal prayer or reflection or, perhaps, a small group's reflection and sharing.

Usually, restaurants will restrict their hors d'oeuvres to a few selections. I offer you more than a few. You have your choice. Some will be familiar and well-known; others will be new and call for your leap of faith.

When I had lunch with my sisters, Jeanne and Alice, often they would order several starters, divide and share, while my sister Rosemary and I would go for a sandwich we particularly enjoyed. Of course, wine was the adult beverage of choice. Perhaps, like my sisters, you might like several hors d'oeuvres and enjoy them for your reflection. Mix, divide, and share.

CONTENTS

A WORLD LIVES IN ME

The Presbyterian theologian and author, Frederick Buechner, wrote:

> "You can kiss your family and friends good-bye and put miles between you, but, at the same time, you carry them with you in your heart, your mind, your stomach, because you do not just live in a world, but the world lives in you."[1]

How true that has been for me! I did kiss my family good-bye in Chicago and put miles between them and myself. I went off to the Vincentian seminary in Missouri where we were not allowed to return home until after ordination to the priesthood: nine years! Yes, the family could come and visit us for one week a year, but we could not leave the seminary grounds, not even to go and have a hamburger with them. Ed, my sister Jeanne's husband, said that it was a "concentration camp." Although the first time I heard his remark, I did not like it; but he had a point.

During those nine years, I missed a lot of family activities, but especially my brother and five sisters growing up. And I missed my mom and stepdad! I waited for letters from my mom which were not as frequent as I would have liked.

I must say, in defense of the seminary, during the first two years -- our novitiate (two-year spiritual boot camp) -- we had to write home once a week. My mom said that she had to have my sisters to translate my poor handwriting! She wrote very clearly.

My priestly assignments also put miles between the family and myself. In the early years of priesthood, we were not allowed to go home for family celebrations, except a funeral of our parents or siblings. My oldest sister, Rosemary, used to haunt me for not being able to witness her marriage. Of course, there was also another problem...little money was available. During my first assignment, I received ten dollars a month for

---

[1] Telling the Truth by Frederick Buechner

my own use. Two dollars of that money went for my monthly haircut; I could get a flattop for that price. The next assignment brought me twenty dollars a month.

What I discovered over the years is: I did carry my family and friends in my heart and mind. I do not just live in a world, but a world lives in me.

I have been blessed over the years. I have lived in different cities of this great world. I have met so many people and made friends in numerous locations. These form the world that lives in me. It is a world to be thankful for. Amazingly, that world keeps expanding.

My family lives from the Bronx to Orange, from Phoenix to Atlanta to Charlotte, from Nashville to Chicago to Milwaukee to Fort Worth.

The world lives in me. People live in me.

What about your world? Does it live in you?

THE SABBATH

I like what the late Pope Benedict XVI said about the Sabbath. I think the insights are thought-provoking and worthy of our reflection.

> "We read in the Book of Genesis that God rested on the seventh day."

As Rabbi Jacob Neusner says:

> "On that day we celebrate creation."
> "Not working on the Sabbath stands for more than nit-picking ritual. It is a way of imitating God."

Those are two positive ways of understanding the Sabbath and celebrating it. The Sabbath is a way of resting. It is not enough merely not to work, but also to rest. Resting means more than just sitting in our favorite chair and munching on chips and dip; it means re-forming family life one day a week: The Sabbath.

The Sabbath is more than a matter of personal piety; it has a social dimension. As Rabbi Neusner says:

> "This day...
> makes eternal Israel what it is, the people that, like God in creating the world, rest from creation on the Seventh Day."

Pope Benedict explored how salutary it would be for our society today if families designated one day a week to stay together and make their home the dwelling place and the fulfillment of communion in God's rest.

Do you agree?

Is the Sabbath just a free day for the mail person or more heavy work?

Does your family enjoy each other's activity on the Sabbath?

Do you have a sit-down special meal together?

HOLY INDIFFERENCE

One day, while in seminary formation, I told Father Dan Martin that I was "holy indifferent" and he shot back, "Then you are a "spiritual coward." Is holy indifference the same as spiritual cowardice? There is a big difference between the two. For one thing, one is positive, the other, negative.

Whether it is "holy" or "wholly" indifference, it involves genuine concern. The concern is to conform as perfectly as possible our will with God's will and be willing to follow that will unconditionally and whole-heartedly. The desired outcome? That our will and God's will coincide. According to Saint Vincent de Paul, that is holiness.

A story from the life of Saint Martin of Tours exemplifies holy indifference.

> Saint Martin called for his brother priests and followers and told them that he was dying. After all, he was 81 years old, and life in rural France had not been easy.
> They reacted immediately. They had a bunch of reasons: You cannot desert us; who will care for us? There are wolves out there that will attack us.
>
> And their clincher (they thought):
> We know that you long to be with Christ, but your reward is certain and will not be any less for being delayed. This touched Saint Martin's heart. He looked to God: "Lord, if your people still need me, I am ready for the task; your will be done."

Death could not defeat him, nor toil dismay him.

He was quite without a preference of his own; he neither feared to die nor refused to live."[2]

Living or Dying – Which One?

---

[2] Epist. 14-17, 21: SC 133, 336-344.

Saint Paul was at that point in his life where he knew in the recesses of his heart that "for to me living is Christ and dying is gain."[3]

Saint Paul had this incredible, personal relationship with the risen Christ. And, besides, he had had a vision of heaven.[4] He knew what was in store for him; there was never any doubt.

The dilemma: which to choose? For Saint Paul, death meant being with Christ Jesus. It meant the end of hardships, pain and suffering, difficulties, and disappointments. Life meant staying alive and continuing his ministry, the mission of Jesus.

A question…Can death be a type of selfishness? Can wanting to die be our desire to escape pain and suffering, hardships, and problems?

I walked into the ICU Unit at Mercy Hospital in St. Louis, MO to see Father Bob Coerver. As soon as he saw me, he said, "Ramson, my bags are packed; I'm ready to go."

"Where are you going? What do you mean, 'Your bags are packed?' Of course, I knew what he meant".

"I am tired of fighting these physical problems; I don't want to go through all this anymore." Bob died shortly after I saw him.

Is the desire to die a type of selfishness? Or does our motive transcend that desire?

"I want to be with Jesus."

Was that Saint Paul's main reason for wanting death?

Is death gain?

---

[3] Philippians 1:21
[4] 2 Corinthians 12:1-10

HUMILITY

When I was a novice, we occasionally had a spiritual exercise called "humiliations" appropriated from our old French rule. It was known among us as "humps."

The idea was to submit ourselves to humiliation. Several of us were chosen by our novice master, Father Jimmy McOwen, to go around and kiss the feet of the other novices arranged in a large semi-circle. Some of the less pious in the bunch would wiggle their toes or move their feet when you came up to kiss their shoes. Novices don't do "humps" anymore and neither do the French.

Humility is not one of the favorite virtues of the modern non-Christian or Christian world. In fact, humility is often considered as a negative virtue rather than a positive one, certainly repressive rather than liberating. The accusation: humility is for wimps! Not many like to eat "humble pie" either.

Why is it that so many shun the very concept of humility, yet are open to humiliation? This is especially true when there is money or minutes of fame involved, e.g., the reality shows or the sitcoms on television. People do not mind being humiliated if it means making a buck or getting their face recognized by millions or getting a few laughs.

There is a big difference between humility and humiliation. What is your choice? I'll take humility.

Yet we hear Jesus tell us, "For everyone who exalts himself will be humbled, but the one who humbles himself will be exalted." (Lk 14:11)

We read in Saint Augustine:

> "Humility is so necessary for Christian perfection that among all the ways to reach perfection, humility is first, humility is second, and humility is third."

What am I hearing? Humility is a *sine qua non* (essential requirement) for anyone serious about the spiritual life.

Thomas Merton says in his classic *New Seeds of Contemplation*:

"It is almost impossible to overestimate the value of true humility and its power in the spiritual life...humility contains in itself the answer to all the great problems of the life of the soul."

The words of Merton that have captivated me for years:

"Humility consists in being precisely the person you actually are before God."

Why is that? I think because humility is the acknowledgement of truth. That is what the saints, like Saint Francis de Sales and Saint Teresa of Avila, tell us. A humble person dwells in the truth. And the truth sets us free.

BEATITUDES

Thirteen years before Pope John Paul beatified Pier Giorgio Frassati, he said:

> "Behold the man of the eight Beatitudes who bears in himself the grace of the gospel, the Good News, the joy of salvation offered to us by Christ."[5]

When he died, Luciana, Pier Giorgio's sister, wrote his biography. In the book, she wrote a chapter on each of the Beatitudes and showed how her brother lived and practiced each one of them. I doubt if any one of my sisters would call me a "Man of the Beatitudes" nor write a biography of me.

Saint Matthew starts off Jesus' Sermon on the Mount with the Beatitudes.

The Beatitudes – the "Be-s." They have everything to do with being. They are attitudes of being. They speak to the inner life of us that is manifested externally.

As one of my now deceased Superior Generals, Father Richard McCullen, C.M. said:

> "Beatitudes are an invasion of God's madness into the world of what humanity considers to be good sense."

Beatitudes are a scale of values. The contemporary world has a difficult time accepting the eight of them. Why would anyone want to label as "blessed" those that are poor in spirit, those who mourn, the meek, those men and women who hunger and thirst for justice, the merciful, the pure of heart, and the peacemakers? Well, maybe, we might concede, and call "peacemakers" blessed in light of the world's confrontations.

The Beatitudes have been called the "Gospel of the Gospel." I read somewhere years ago that some scholars believed if the entire New

---

[5] Cracoviam March 27, 1977

Testament was lost and the only fragment left for humanity was the Beatitudes, the world would have a clear and precise idea of who Jesus Christ was.

The Beatitudes also have been described as a self-portrait of Jesus. The Beatitudes have been described as the Charter, the Constitutions of the Kingdom of Heaven.

Another deceased vincentian, the great scripture scholar, Father Bruce Vawter, wrote:

> "The Sermon of the Mount is not a collection of idealis-
> tic poetry but a proclamation of Christian values and a
> realistic exhortation to a standard virtue that is possible
> only through the power given by the Spirit of God."

What would you list as your eight Beatitudes? Can you come up with eight?

FATHER NICHOLAS KALOKI, C.M.

I live in a retirement facility for Vincentian priests and brothers. Since I arrived, I have witnessed several deaths and burials in our community cemetery.

Recently, our confreres in Kenya sent Father Nicholas to us. He was suffering from liver cancer. I knew Nicholas from his first days as a seminary student because I was a formator at our seminary in Karen, just outside of Nairobi. Nicholas had just celebrated his thirty-ninth birthday when he came to us in the United States; he would never see his fortieth.

He sat with me at table during meals. When he remained in his room, I visited several times a day. He eventually gave up eating. Our nursing staff took extremely good care of him.

Nicholas never complained about anything, including pain. The only time he showed pain was when the nurses would turn him in bed to prevent bed sores.

Members of our community prayed the rosary at his bedside in the evening. At first Nicholas fingered his beads, but then he became too ill to do that.

He called me "Babu" which means "grandfather" in Kiswahili. It is a term of endearment.

Toward the end of his life, I would sit in his room in silence and ask Nicholas (in silence): "Nicholas, what are you teaching us, what are you teaching Babu?"

Inevitably, I received ideas, thoughts. I attributed them to the promptings of the Holy Spirit. But I can't leave Nicholas out of the picture because he was the one I asked the question: "Nicholas, what are you teaching us?"

I have not cried, in my many years of priestly ministry, as I have over Nicholas. He was like a brother to me. To witness a Vincentian priest, die at such a young age was heart-wrenching!

The first time I gave him the Sacrament of the Sick, he cried. I had to leave his room. I completely lost it. Amazingly, the day he died, I was rubbing his right arm, while Sidney, the hospice nurse, was talking to

Nicholas on the other side of the bed. Sidney said, "Father Nicholas, today you are going to see Jesus." I didn't cry until the next day.

I want to thank God for the grace that I received: to be present when Nicholas died. It is a gift that many don't ever experience.

Father Nicholas had a great devotion to Saint Padre Pio. We got a twelve-inch statue of the saint and turned it toward Nicholas. I prayed that Padre Pio take care of my brother. I told a couple of nurses, if they saw a stranger in Father Nicholas' room, not to be surprised. Padre Pio is noted for appearing to the dying.

Nicholas died at thirty-nine years old, seven years a priest.

When no one was around, I asked Nicholas as he laid in his coffin: "Have you and Padre Pio talked?" I just talked to him as if he were present in his room.

What did Father Nicholas teach us – teach me?

- Compassion--individual and communal
- Courage
- Never complain about pain
- He allowed me to express my inner feelings like never before

Our Kenyan mission wanted a healthy Nicholas to return to them, but God wanted him.

Nicholas amazed the nurses and us in how he fought the fight to the end.

DEPARTED

The older I get, the more I think of death -- my death. I was in danger three times recently. I received the Sacrament of the Sick several times this past year.

Saint Vincent de Paul said:

> "All our life is but a moment which flies away and disappears quickly...the years of my life which I have passed, seem to me but a dream and a moment."

Do I see my life as a dream and a moment, or a nightmare and a slow-moving movie?

Catholics, like many others, Christian and non-Christian, pray for their loved ones. As we pray, we remember that "Life is changed, not ended." Blood relationships never die, although friendships might.

Praying for the dead and to the dead is an important part of the grieving process. We continue to deepen our love for the deceased as we remember them in prayer after their death. Each of us has a necrology.

After all these years, I still think of my mother who died at forty-two. How I wish that she was physically alive, and that I could sit down with her and tell her about what is going on in my life. I can't do that, but I can still talk to her. I can still pray for her; she can still pray for me. The same goes for my stepdad who raised me and my deceased brother Bill and sisters, Beverly Ann, Lucille, Jeanne – and my grandparents and godparents.

I inscribed a bunch of names in our "Book of the Dead" this past year. Praying for the dead reminds us that death is not an end, but a beginning of new life. Isn't life but a conglomeration of beginnings and ends?

On the back of our Vincentian ordo (read calendar) it says: "Members who have migrated back to the heavenly homeland." Our deceased loved ones have migrated to heaven.

May the souls of the faithful departed rest in peace.

FAITH

Father Paul O'Malley came into my room in Chicago and sat on the edge of my bed. He was a priest in his eighties and had had a tough life with a lot of sickness. I personally thought he was a man of deep spirituality.

> He said, "Can I ask you a question?
> Do you ever have doubts about the faith?
> I do."

> And I, in the arrogance of early priesthood, replied, "No, not really."

> Now, after all these years, how I would like to have the opportunity to answer him: "Yes, Paul, I also have doubts about faith, especially about afterlife."

One of my favorite prayers is that of the father whose son has epilepsy:

> "I believe; help my unbelief!"[6]

Saint Augustine once said, "Faith is to believe what you do not see; the reward of this faith is to see what you believe."

I think that too many people say they have faith, but don't. Too many say: "Show me, and I'll believe." But God says: "No, believe, and then I'll show you."

We get it backwards.

Belief comes first.

---

[6] Mark 9: 24

TICK-TUCK

How many times did I hear Peter, Paul, and Mary sing: "Time is a wasting?"

And many times I have read or heard Jesus say:

> "You also must be prepared, for at an hour you do not
> expect, the Son of Man will come."[7]

The Church invites us to think ahead. The Gospel gives us flashing warning signs: Be prepared! Stay awake! And we can't, in all honesty, say that we don't have every opportunity to be ready. Jesus has given us the sacraments, especially Confession, the Eucharist, and Anointing of the Sick.

The Sacrament of Penance is the sacrament of compassion. God forgives us when we come before him with sincerity and contrition. The Eucharist is the source, center, and summit of the spiritual life. The healing Jesus consoles and comforts us in our suffering and illness.

Jesus gave us his Mother also as a gift. The seven sacraments are gifts. Mother Mary is a gift. The Church is a gift. The list goes on. How many gifts do we need to be and stay prepared?

What do we want? Maybe, a personal, printed invitation hand-delivered by an angel?

---

[7] Matthew 24:44

GOD AND I TALK

You probably heard the classic episode from the life of the Cure of Ars, Saint Jean-Marie Vianney. Jean-Marie had seen this old man in one of the back pews of the parish church. It appeared that he said nothing and read nothing. He just sat there for long periods of time. Finally, out of curiosity, the saint asked the old man:

> "What do you do? You just sit here for long periods of time."
> The senior answered, "I look at him; he looks at me."

In other words, the old timer had this fabulous relationship going on between God and himself. He did not need a prayer book or a rosary, just himself. It was the type of prayer that many would give their eye teeth for. I would have enjoyed speaking to this man and learning what he had heard over the years. What did God say to him? What was the conversation?

A vital part of prayer is listening and allowing God to speak to us. Too often, too many of us make time for prayer, but use all the time by filling it with reciting prayers, preventing God from getting a word in edgewise. We think that is what God wants: monologues from us, as if we finite creatures can provide God with beautiful and new thoughts.

Are we trying to impress God? Is this subtle pride?

I think that the old Frenchman from Ars, probably was not well educated, but he knew what authentic prayer was. He discovered the secret of prayer: we learn how to pray by praying.

Monologues make good show business, not good prayer. Dialogues do.

FROM A DISTANCE

There is a song composed by Julie Gold often played on the FM stations: *From a Distance*. I like the melody, and some of the lyrics sound like they could have come from one of the prophetic books of the Bible, perhaps the prophet Isaiah.

From a distance, the world is beautiful, there is peace and harmony, everyone has enough to eat, and we are unified playing songs of hope and peace. From a distance, you look like my friend, so why are we at war? There are certainly themes of the prophets here, especially when we hear: "It's the hope of hopes, it's the love of loves."

Ms. Julie Gold has stated that she believes in an imminent and beneficent God, and thinks that people have a right to interpret the song any way they want, as with all art. My interpretation is that the song rings with some bad theology and bad spirituality. Yes, "God is watching us" but not merely from a distance. That is not what we Christians believe.

It is not God over there, and we are here. There is not the separation of God and us. We believe that God dwells within us. We believe that the Triune God dwells within us when we live in a state of sanctifying grace.

Besides, is that all God is doing, watching us? And is there no connection, no interrelationship? Where and when does divine providence come into the picture?

Is God sitting back and watching us live it out, fight it out?

Oh, yes, we believe that God created us, but now what?

Are we on our own as if God says, "Good luck! See you after you die?"

No! God is with us now and always!

CIVILITY

What ever happened to civility? Is it only a word in the dictionary without a matching reality? What happened to it? It is missing in the chambers of legislatures. It is missing among membership of churches. Have we so divided ourselves as to cause irreconcilable differences?

I have never experienced such incivility in my life as I have in these recent years.

I heard a celebrity on a talk show, someone I never expected, say this about incivility:

> "It's what we have become. People think that now we must be nasty."

Is this true? Do people think that incivility is now the expected norm among people in public office, in politics?

The Jewish Council of Public Affairs said:

> "Civility is neither the lack of difference nor the squelching of debate. It is the application of care for the dignity of every human being, even those with whom we may sharply disagree."

Some of the Catholic hierarchy have called for civility. Read persons like Timothy Michael Cardinal Dolan and Kevin Cardinal Farrell before they got the red hats.

Prelates will say very clearly that calling for civility and moderation does not compromise our faith and teachings, but it does mean that we treat each other with respect as befits our dignity and avoid personal attacks.

One bishop commends efforts to restore civility to our national dialogue and in our daily life. Archbishop Dolan, then Archbishop of Milwaukee, in an address to the State Legislature of Wisconsin, said that civility is the cement that keeps a respectful, trusting, productive society and community focused and fruitful.

The prelate noted the three foundations of civility: self-respect, respect for others, and a commonsense conclusion that society can only survive, prosper, and fulfill its purpose if it is well-ordered by virtue and responsibility.

What is the relationship between civility and civil, between civility and citizen?

VIRTUE STANDS IN THE MIDDLE

I gave a talk to the Downtown Dallas Serra Club and chose the topic: "In Medio Stat Virtus" – *Virtue Stands in the Middle.*

I expressed my concerns: church and state are both getting more and more polarized. How much more polarized can they get before exploding at the ends of the continuum? Is that possible?

Whatever happened to the middle? Have we lost it completely and forever? I thought that the church has been the church of the middle. Not anymore.

I listen to Catholic radio stations, I listen to talk-radio, I watch Catholic television, I watch television talk programs, and I hear and see polarization. People are digging in at the extremes. We have lost our middle. As several businesspeople have pointed out to me, who wants to watch or listen to some person in the middle? It does not sell. The media wants explosions and outrageous statements.

Sister Joan Chittister wrote that "we have become a society of opposites" – and perhaps, "a society at war with itself."

Will we – can we – ever recover a middle? Or are we too long gone – passed fail safe?

Yet look at the great ancient philosophers; look at the saints. They never speak to us about virtue in the extremes, but only in the middle.

Love is the eternal virtue. As we read in Saint Paul: "And now faith, hope, and love abide, these three; and the greatest of these is love."[8] In heaven, there is no faith, no hope, because you don't need them. Only love.

Can we have too little love? I suspect the general consensus would be: yes. Can we have too much love? What would be the consensus? How many would vote yes, how many no? But we can and do have extremes in virtues.

Aristotle defined a virtue as a balance point between a deficiency and an excess of a trait. The point of greatest virtue lies not in the exact middle, as you might think, but he saw it as a golden mean, sometimes closer

---

[8] I Corinthians 13:13

to one extreme than the other. I think that our human experience would confirm that idea. For example, courage is the mean between courage on one end of the spectrum and recklessness on the other extreme; confidence the mean between self-deprecation and vanity; generosity the mean between complete stinginess and extravagance. We can see the same pattern with any virtue.

But do you really believe that virtue stands in the middle? Or, do you see it only in extremes?

HEART

I have enjoyed Broadway musicals ever since I was a teenager. Perhaps it is due to my mother. She was in show business – a professional dancer and had been a member of a troop that toured parts of the country. One of my memories was my mother teaching me how to play castanets. The pair was of rather highly polished black ebony joined by a red cord. I never did well with them; occasionally I would take them out from her cedar chest and try to make the clicking noise.

The last time that I saw Jerry Ross and Richard Adler's *Damn Yankees* it brought back good memories of the original cast. One of the memorable songs is:

> "You've gotta have heart. All you really need is heart.
> You've gotta have hope! Mustn't sit around and mope."

How true is that? We must have heart. And moping gets us nowhere.

In the ecclesial quarters we do not say "heart;" we call it fortitude or, if you prefer, courage. No matter what we call it, we need it in life especially when things are not going well.

Henri Nouwen wrote in *Reaching Out*:

> "Among the many great spiritual men and women of history, we may find a few or maybe just one or two who speak the language of our heart and give us courage. These are our guides."

The question of the day: Who speaks the language of your heart? Who gives you courage?

Saint Vincent de Paul taught: "first the heart, then the work." That is more than an operating principle, it is a life principle. Our heart comes first, then the work. Isn't that reasonable, logical?

What makes us respond or act when we see someone suffering or in need? What makes us go to their assistance? Isn't it first our heart?

Compassion kicks in. Compassion is an active verb. Don't just think of it as a noun.

HOPE

I took French for two years in college and our professor, Father Leo Ebisch, C.M., introduced us to some of the great French authors. One was Charles Peguy who wrote a poem about the virtues, in which the narrator is Father God. He says about hope:

> "Ah, hope, my little daughter, my little girl running on
> and playing in front of me in the world.
> Little hope, so fragile, so frail, but she's always there."

One of the best things I have seen on hope was a quote from another Frenchman, Blessed Frederic Ozanam:

> "Hope! The fault of many Christians these days is that
> they hope too little. At every struggle, at every obstacle,
> they believe it is the downfall of the Church. They are
> the apostles in the boat during the storm; they forget
> that the Savior is with them. They forget that all ages of
> the Church have had plenty of perils to cause people to
> fear, but there has been plenty of help to cause people to
> hope. Catholicism, which in our days still has its storms,
> also has its reassuring signs."[9]

The anchor is one of the ancient Christian symbols. It symbolizes hope. Hope is the anchor of our personal lives and the lives of our communities.

"We have this hope, a sure and steadfast anchor of the soul..."[10]

The purpose of an anchor is to fix the boat, the ship, the barque, to one position. A boat can easily drift in water due to currents, rising tides, and storms. Our hope in Jesus keeps us anchored to him, our eyes fixed on him.[11]

---

[9] Ozanam: Letter # 599, Dominique Meynis, January 29, 1845 (The author's translation)
[10] Hebrews 6:19
[11] Hebrews 12:2

When assailed by temptations, when storms arise in our lives, when waters of life become choppy, hope is our anchor.

Cardinal Francois Xavier Nguyen van Thuan once said:

"Not infrequently do we feel we are losers in the modern world. But the adventure of hope takes us beyond."

ATTACK THE ISSUE, NOT THE PERSON

Look at the political commercials. Listen or look at the debates and talk shows and what do we hear and see? Attacks on the person. Opponents are not content with addressing the issue, so they do a number on the person, which, sometimes, includes the candidate's family. A bummer!

A thirty-seven-year-old married French Catholic, a professor at the Sorbonne, Frederic Ozanam, wrote this:

> "Let us learn much! Let us learn principally to defend our convictions without hating our adversaries, to love those who think differently than us, to recognize that there are Christians in all camps and that God can be served today as always! Let us complain less of our time and more of ourselves; let us be less discouraged but let us be better."[12]

Does it take heroic charity for a politician to stick to the issue and not attack the person in the other camp?

Does it take heroic charity for a Catholic to stick to the issue and not attack the Catholic with a different viewpoint in the other camp?

Does it take heroic charity for any Christian to stick with the issue and not attack the other person of another religion or no religion?

I am beginning to think the answer is yes.

Am I wrong?

---

[12] Letter 1069, April 9, 1851

SCRIPTURE ROULETTE

I made my annual retreat in Cincinnati in the house of Father Richard Rohr, OFM, a well-known Franciscan. One day, he handed me a note: "Ron, call this number; it is important." I looked at the number and for the life of me, I had no idea who was calling me.

It turned out to be my provincial. "Ron, we would like you to go to Chicago as an associate pastor, and work with the Spanish-speaking." I was stunned because on my desk back in Cotulla, Texas there was a letter appointing me to St. Leo's, San Antonio. My immediate response was: "If that is what the community wants, okay."

Then I did something that I never recommend to anyone. I went to the chapel, which then had no chairs or pews, sat on the floor, and opened up a bible at random. I was playing scripture roulette.

I prayed, "Lord, give me a sign that Chicago is indeed your will for me."

Guess where I opened up the bible? It was Chapter 10, the Letter to the Hebrews. I started to read:

> "Then I said, 'See, God, I have come to do your will, O God.'" And further, once again: "See, I have come to do your will."

I eventually took over as pastor at Saint Vincent de Paul Church, and, I must say, in all honesty, that I always had the deep conviction that this ministry was God's will for me. It was not my easiest assignment, but it opened me up to various works and wonderful people. Our Spanish Masses were the largest in attendance, with a varied array of Mexicans, Puerto Ricans, Central Americans, and a sprinkling of those from South America.

I made a Cursillo with several confreres. I got involved in Marriage Encounter which only enhanced my own celibate vocation.

These played an important part of life.

MAGI

I have been blessed over the years with "wisdom people" – Magi – men and women who have gifted me by their gifts of wisdom, street smarts, and good common sense.

I think of Iggy, Ruth, Greg, Judy, Howie, Rosalie, Jeanne, Vincent, Ed, Rita, Sidney, Leo, Liz, Joe, Nancy, Jim – to name but a few. My Magi came from different corners of the world, into my world, representatives of different vocations and careers.

Two things stand out in the lives of canonized saints:

1. They surrounded themselves with wise and holy people of both genders. Even a cursory glance of their biographies shows this.
2. Behind every great man is a great woman, and saints are no exception. We have: Augustine and Monica, Francis and Clare, Benedict and Scholastica, Vincent de Paul and Louise de Marillac, Frederic and Amelie, Francis de Sales and Jeanne-Francoise de Chantal and list goes on.

In many cases, these pairs were collaborators in works of God. In all cases, they nourished each other, challenged each other, and certainly were mutual exemplars.

What gets some of us human beings in trouble, in serious trouble, is hanging around with the wrong crowd – with men and women not wise and holy.

Who are the Magi in your life – living and dead?

POUSTINIA

During my time as pastor in Cotulla, Texas, I learned much about myself among those God-blessed people. I call it my "desert experience" or "poustinia" using the terminology of Baroness Catherine de Hueck Doherty.

"Poustinia" is a Russian word meaning *desert*. In her book the Baroness writes about encountering God in silence, solitude, and prayer. The book spoke to my heart and was most apropos at that time of my life. I was happy to see that the book was awarded the prestigious French Academy Award and endorsed by Dorothy Day and Father Edward J. Farrell.

I experienced poustinia in Cotulla. It was not an easy assignment for a bunch of reasons, but, as Saint Vincent de Paul says, "Grace has its moments." Cotulla was one of those moments.

Two minor challenges were avoiding the bats flying around my head at early morning Mass and occasionally killing good-sized scorpions on the floor of the church.

I learned more Sacred Scripture there than I had during my days in the seminary! I listened to tapes. I studied Scripture more than ever before. Father Richard Rohr, O.F.M. was a favorite of mine.

A great blessing for me was conducting a bible study group at Ruth Maltsberger's house. Ruth was one of my Magi. I learned much in my preparations for the weekly classes and from the women in attendance. They were of all faiths: Church of Christ, Baptist, Anglican, and Catholic, but the majority were Protestant.

I was following in the footsteps of a well-loved priest, Father Dennis Flynn. Denny had taught me English Composition in high school. He had taught for some years at De Paul University in Chicago; he treated us teens more like collegians than high school kids. He demanded that we write paragraphs daily. He would tell us what he wanted. We turned them in, and we got the homework back with his comments. I think that I can trace my liking for writing to his classes.

When I was transferred from Cotulla, the women of the Bible class surprised me with a gorgeous hand-made, author-signed, copper plague.

It was entitled: "Paisano" which means *countryman,* but in Texas it means *roadrunner.* The plaque shows a roadrunner, a common sight in south-central Texas. It hangs on my bedroom wall. I was honored and touched by the ladies' gift!

They gave me more than I gave them.

YEAST

Our students at our minor Seminary in Beaumont, Texas were having a party for Halloween and wanted to make pizzas from scratch. I told them that I would buy the dough to save them some time and make it easier on their cooks.

I bought the dough from a professional baking company; they put the dough in a cardboard box, closed the lid, and placed it on the front seat of my car.

As I was driving back to the seminary down the interstate, the top of the box popped open and scared me to death. Coming out was a mass of dough. With one hand on the steering wheel, I punch down the dough and closed the lid. Again, it popped open, and more dough started to come forth like lava from a volcano. It was like something from a scary Si-Fi movie. Was the dough going to take over my front seat? It was eerie!

I finally got back to the school and turned the growing dough mass over to the students with the recommendation: "You better put this in the frig."

Yeast – leaven – Jesus compares the kingdom of heaven to yeast that a woman took and mixed in with three measures of flour until all of it was leavened.[13]

Yeast penetrates, permeates. The kingdom of heaven begins in us, with us. Then we go out to others. But the "yeast" must do its magic in us first. Are we open to the yeast, the yeast of God?

Yeast, like salt and light that Jesus talks about, are servant images. Nobody makes a meal out of yeast. We eat bread raised by yeast.

Let us beware of the yeast of the scribes and Pharisees.

---

[13] Mt 13:33 or Lk 13:20-21

BELIEVE OR BELIEVE IN?

"In" is a very small word; we call it a preposition, but it is a word that packs a lot of whoop.

Samuel Coleridge said that he believed Plato and Socrates, but he believed "in" Jesus Christ. That little "in" says much more when attached to "believe."

"In" suggests a leap, an insertion, a movement of confidence and abandon. It may even suggest something more grandiose: a personal commitment to the God who calls us.

What do we say as a community of faith in our churches? "I believe in one God, the Father almighty..." ("Credo in unum Deo....") I believe in. I do not merely believe the following twelve statements, but I believe in them.

A famous Dominican spiritual author of years ago, Gerald Vann, shocked his contemporaries at a time when shocking was not vogue:

> "I don't believe in dogmas, doctrines, and teachings of the Catholic Church; I believe through them in the living reality beyond – in the person of Jesus."

Of course, we do believe the dogmas, doctrines, and the teachings of the Church, but we believe in Jesus. We believe many things, many truths, but we believe in a person, and this Person is Jesus Christ, God-man.

There is a difference between believe and believe in.

How do you see it?

CLARITY OR TRUST?

Father John F. Kavanaugh, a Jesuit priest, taught at Saint Louis University. Some years before (now Saint) Mother Teresa of Calcutta died, Father Kavanaugh spent a month at the "House of Dying" in Calcutta, India with Mother's community, The Missionary Sisters of Charity. Father Kavanaugh told this story on himself. Perhaps you have heard it:

> At the time, Father was in a discernment mode. He was looking at his future and was seeking an answer. He wanted something clear, clean-cut.
>
> He met Mother Teresa at the center, and she, gracious as always, asked him: "What can I do for you?" And Father answered: "Pray for me."
>
> "What do you want me to pray for?"
>
> "What I have wanted most of all: pray that I may have clarity."
>
> And Mother Teresa fired back: "No."
>
> The priest was surprised and not too well-pleased with the negative response.
>
> "Why will you not pray that I may have clarity for my future?"
>
> "Clarity is the last thing that you are clinging to, and you have to let go of it."
>
> Father, a bit defensive, said: "You yourself always seem to have the clarity that I long for." Mother Teresa laughed.

"I have never had clarity; what I have always had is trust.
So, I will pray that you trust."

How many of us want clarity in our lives, in everything we do, in everything we are planning to do? We want things understandable; we want certainty, and not doubt, confusion, or ambiguity. A tall order!

Life is not always so neat and tidy and crystal clear. There are too many detours, stormy days, obstacles, and setbacks. We all have our stories: illnesses, trips to the emergency room, a heart attack, gallbladder or gut flare-ups....

As Jesus said to Thomas:

"Blessed are those who have not seen and yet believe."[14]

---

[14] John 20:29

I THIRST

I gave the vow retreat to the novices of the Missionary Sisters of Charity at their formation house in one of the large slums of Nairobi, Kenya. The retreat lasted eight days but I stayed ten. During the night, I could hear the babies crying in the building opposite my room. These were the babies with various physical deformities that the Sisters cared for, precious in the eyes of God!

During the night, I also heard the guard dogs moving around and occasionally fighting among themselves. The Sisters released the dogs before retiring for the night. The dogs were so bad that only certain Sisters could handle them, and they had to divide the dogs into two groups and keep them separated in different parts of the compound. I could never leave my room until 5:00 am, after the Sisters had collected the dogs.

Every day I went into chapel for communal prayer and conferences and squatting on the floor before me were the novices and their Novice Mistresses. Outside the doors, there was an assortment of varied colored flip-flops and sandals. The Sisters told me to keep my shoes on, but I decided to join the club.

Behind me, as I talked, on the chapel wall, was a huge crucifix and next to it were the words "I thirst."

Jesus said:

> "Let anyone who is thirsty come to me and let the one
> who believes in me drink."[15]

As Jesus was dying on the cross, he was dying of dehydration also. He thirsts for cool drinking water. But he was thirsting for us as well – dying for our salvation – thirsting for our souls.

People in the pews are thirsty; students in the universities are thirsty. They all want to be sated with the living waters of Jesus Christ.

---

[15] John 7:37

"Those who drink of the water that I will give them will never be thirsty.
The water that I will give will become in them a spring of water gushing up to eternal life."[16]

Are we thirsty for Jesus?

---

[16] John 4:14

TWO HEROES

Two people that I have admired are Dom Helder Camara, the famous archbishop from Brazil, and Mother Teresa of Calcutta. Both are deceased but very much alive in the minds of many of us.

I think that I have been attracted to these people because of a similar spirituality. From what I have read, they taught and lived much of the tenets of the same spirituality which I hold dear...the spirituality of Saint Vincent de Paul with its charism for the poor.

During the Eucharistic Congress in Philadelphia in 1976 the two were invited to appear on a television show. They accepted the invitation. When Archbishop Camara arrived, Mother Teresa was already there. She said to him:

> "O Dom Helder, I remember how beautifully you described the way you protect yourself when you enter an auditorium filled with people who are giving you a standing ovation. I remember how you pray, 'Lord Jesus, this is your triumphal entry into Jerusalem. I will be your little donkey.' That has really helped me."

And Dom Helder immediately replied:

> "I am trying to protect myself from the pride of humility."

What does that mean? Can we be proud of our humility? I think so. I remember a verse of Mac Davis' song:

> "Oh Lord it's hard to be humble
>
> when you're perfect in every way.
>
> I can't wait to look in the mirror

'cos I get better looking each day.

*To know me is to love me…"

Both Archbishop Camara and Mother Teresa were walking exemplars of humility.
Sometimes we forget that humility is found in true greatness.

BASEBALL: A GAME OF FAILURE

I like baseball a lot. I enjoy the sport more than any other. One of the great advantages of cable/satellite TV is the accessibility of ball games!

The first professional game I ever saw was when I was in eighth grade at Mozart Public School in Chicago. Mr. Cusimano took his son, my classmate, Frank, and me to see the Chicago White Sox vs. the Boston Red Sox. We had a great pasta dinner before we left the house thanks to grandma Cusimano. A long street-ride to old Comiskey Park followed.

The White Sox have been my team for years, although I have seen other teams more frequently. I like the newer ballparks in Denver, St. Louis, Baltimore, and San Francisco.

The one striking thing about baseball is that it is a game of failure. Minor and Major league players must not only understand this, but accept it.

If a player hits for a 333 average, that means that he is getting only one hit for every four times at bat. Now 333 is an excellent batting average at the end of any season. Not many professional ballplayers do that well!

Baseball is one of the few games where errors and strikeouts are recorded. When you watch a game – or play a game – you expect some player will make an error or strike out. Those are failures on their part. Baseball players get big money for failure, presumably, more money for less failure. What other professional sports pay extravagant salaries for failure?

How do we handle failures in life? Can we handle them? Some people have a difficult time doing so. This is where trust comes in. This is where God's grace comes in.

David Foster, the famous musician, composer, and producer said in an interview:

> "Failure is not an option. Failure is energizing. When you get blocked, stay with it. Live it, breathe it, eat it, sleep it."

Baseball is a game of failure, but not life.
Ask Jesus.

WRESTLING WITH GOD

The famous Greek author, Nikos Kazantzakis, recounts a conversation he had with a senior monk, Father Makarios.

Kazantzakis asked the monk:

"Do you still wrestle with the devil, Father Makarios?"

The priest sighed and answered:

"Not any longer, my child. I have grown old now, and he has grown old with me. He does not have the strength...I wrestle with God."

And Kazantzakis was astonished:

"With God! And you hope to win?"

"I hope to lose, my child. My bones remain with me still, and they continue to resist."

With whom are we wrestling? God, the devil, or ourselves? Do we fight with all three?

Does it depend on our age? Our battles change opponents in teens, adulthood, and senior years. At least, I think so.

Does it depend on the status of our spiritual life?

We all have our own salvation history, and we all have our own sin history; they are linear. I think that our dominant sins do not change in life, but they do become more subtle.

DOES SOCIAL JUSTICE = SOCIALISM?

A well-known TV personality told Christians:

> "I beg you, look for the words 'social justice' or 'economic justice' on your church's website. If you find it, run as fast as you can."

To this man, social justice and economic justice are secret code words. If your parish priest is advocating social justice, you should find another parish. My advice...Don't move!

As you can imagine, this personality's words left some Catholics confused. The Catholic Church has promoted social justice for centuries. Look at the prophet Amos. Look at some of the holy ones, Saint Vincent de Paul and Blessed Frederic Ozanam. Look at the papal encyclicals starting with *Rerum Novarum* of Leo XIII and then those of John Paul II.

There is quite a difference between social justice and socialism. You would think that any celebrity host would do his homework and know the difference, instead of shooting from the hip.

Socialism is defined as economic or political theories that advocate collective or governmental ownership and administration of the means of production and distribution of goods.

What's the threat of socialism? It threatens the identity of the individual because it merges the masses into one common goal or voice.

Social justice is a different ball game. It isn't an economic or political theory, but an outlook that seeks to strengthen the identity of the individual because it sees that human dignity derives its meaning from being made in the image and likeness of God. In God's image we are all equal in worth. All are deserving of life and whatever is needed to adequately sustain it.

During our former community eight-day retreats, the first two meditations were on creation and conversation. I would now include social justice under that latter meditation.

Social justice means living in right relationship. A classic definition of justice is giving everyone what is due to them, and that includes God. We must live justly not only with God, but with our neighbor next door and all humanity.

While socialism is seen as a threat to individual identity, social justice is a call to honor the life and dignity of each person, especially the least of our brothers and sisters (see Matthew 25).

1 + 1 = 2 Social justice does not = socialism.

IT IS TIME TO SOAR

The famous Danish philosopher, Soren Kierkegaard, once told the story about a make-believe land where only ducks lived.

One Sunday morning all the ducks came into church, waddled down the aisle, waddled into their pews and squatted. Then the duck minister came into the sanctuary, took his place in the pulpit, opened the Duck Bible and read:

> "Ducks! You have wings, and with wings you can fly like eagles. You can soar the skies! Ducks! You have wings!
> All the ducks yelled "Amen!" and then they waddled home.
> No one flew; not one tried to fly.

> Those who wait for the Lord shall renew their strength,
> they shall mount up with wings like eagles,
> they shall run and not be weary,
> they shall walk and not faint.[17]

As that well-known and frequently sung song by Michael Joncas reads:

> "And He will raise you up on eagle's wings,
> Bear you on the breath of dawn,
> Make you to shine like the sun,
> And hold you in the palm of His hand."

What Jesus teaches is that it is time to stop waddling; it is time to soar like the eagles.

So, who are we?

Ducks that can fly but won't, or eagles that soar?

The choice is ours.

---

[17] Isaiah 40:31

CHRISTMAS BEGINS

Howard Thurman died in San Francisco April 10, 1981. He has been described as a preacher, teacher, scholar, author, poet, and mystic. He was an inspiration to the civil rights movement of the 50's and 60's and helped to introduce the ideals of nonviolence as promoted by Mahatma Gandhi.

Thurman advocated a "liberation theology" long before the term became well-known in theological circles. I read that "he worked behind the scenes, carefully putting together a theology that would reconcile the struggles of the civil rights era with the spiritual concerns of the church."

Howard Thurman has written one of my favorite prayers for the Christmas season – and the days after...

> "When the song of the angels is stilled,
> when the star in the sky is gone,
> when the kings and princes are home,
> when the shepherds are back with their flock,
> the work of Christmas begins:
> to find the lost,
> to heal the broken,
> to feed the hungry,
> to release the prisoner,
> to rebuild the nations,
> to bring peace among others,
> to make music in the heart."

I hope that you will find great consolation in these words.

I recommend that you read more of this great personage: Howard Thurman.

CHALK ON THE DOOR

Many of us know the story of the Passover. Moses told the people:

> "When he (the Lord) sees the blood on the lintel and on the two doorposts, the Lord will pass over that door and will not allow the destroyer to enter your houses to strike you down."[18]

Today, observant Jews use the mezuzah on their doorways – a small container in which is a piece of parchment on which is written the Schema prayer: "Hear, O Israel, the Lord our God, the Lord is one!"[19] It is customary for Jews to touch the mezuzah on entering the house as a reminder of God's presence there.

Many Catholics have a small holy water font on the wall outside a room or at the entrance of the church or chapel from which they take water blessed by the priest or deacon and then make the sign of the cross before entering that space.

There is a custom at Epiphany to use chalk. With chalk, Catholics write symbols on the main doorframes of their homes to seek the blessings of God for the coming New Year. I remember doing it in Denver at our house of formation. Traditionally, with chalk, one inscribes "C, M, B" (the traditional names of the Magi: Caspar, Melchior, and Balthazar). It is a reminder that everyone who lives in this place also follows Jesus. "CMB" may also stand for the Latin phrase: "Christus Mansionem Benedicat" – *May Christ bless this house.* Some people will write the old year in chalk on the left side of the CMB and the new year of the right side.

Why chalk? It is a substance made from common elements of earth and is used by teachers to instruct students on the blackboards and used by children in their games and play on the sidewalks. The purpose of the chalking: we let the world know what we believe in and whom we follow.

---

[18] Exodus 12:13
[19] Deuteronomy 6:4

THE CHILEAN MINERS

Remember that incredible story of the Chilean miners? More than a mile underground in the Chilean mine, Jimmy Sanchez, age 19, sent up a letter:

> "There are actually 34 of us here; God has never left us down here."

While the media from around the world had discussions with experts focusing on drilling and technology, many of the Chilean miners were focusing on God.

Mario Supulveda said:

> "I was with God, and I was with the devil, and God won."

I am sure there were battles between despair and hope waging in the minds of the 33 miners: 32 Chileans and 1 Bolivian.

What surfaces time and time again in the gospels: God has never left us.

> "The Word became flesh and pitched his tent among us."[20]

And he has never dismantled that tent. It is still with us. Emmanuel, God with us.

As the old poster read:

> "When God seems distant, who moved?"

Saint Paul urges us:

> "Stand firm in the Lord."[21]

---

[20] John 1:14
[21] Philippians 4:1

LENT AND RAMADAN

I was blessed and gave a talk at a Catholic Boys' High School in a slum of Nairobi, Kenya. The school was not large by our American standards, but still it had a good number; approximately 125 of the teens were Muslims. Many Muslim families send their boys to a Catholic high school for a bunch of reasons, probably for the same as parents in the United States.

What to talk about? Because of the appropriateness, I talked about Ramadan and Lent. I found a very receptive audience.

Ramadan and Lent have similarities. Both seasons are marked by prayer, fasting, and charity. Ramadan lasts for one month, while our Lent goes forty days.

The Muslims practice fasting while the sun shines: no food, no water until sunset. That alone is quite an accomplishment. The teen boys always impressed me by their ability to fast. It was a challenge for any Catholic!

Fasting serves many purposes. While they are hungry and thirsty, Muslims are reminded of the suffering of the poor and less fortunate. Fasting is also an opportunity to practice self-control and to cleanse the inner soul and free it from harm. Fasting is an act of deep personal worship to seek a higher level of closeness to Allah. These purposes for a Muslim are not much different for a Catholic. But instead of Allah, we fast in honor of the suffering and death of our Lord, Jesus.

The Qur'an mentions Jesus – "Isa" in Arabic – some 25 times. "Isa" is a servant of Allah, a messenger of Allah, a prophet, the son of Mary, but not divine in their thinking.

During Ramadan, the Muslims attempt to practice charity with greater emphasis on refraining from anger, violence, envy, greed, lust, gossip, etc. They are meant to be more charitable with each other. Purity of both thought and action is important also.

Prayer, fasting, and charity, and the greatest of these is charity.

THE DRIVING FORCE

What is it that motivates us, drives us?

Money? Power? Reputation? A lousy self-image? What is the driving force of our lives? Perhaps there are more than one?

There is a statement attributed to the deceased Superior General of the Jesuits, Pedro Arrupe:

> "Nothing is more practical than finding God, that is, falling in love in a quite absolute final way.
> What you are in love with, what seizes your imagination will affect everything.
> It will decide what will get you out of the bed in the morning, what you do with your weekends, what you read, who you know, what breaks your heart and what amazes you with joy and gratitude.
> Fall in love, stay in love and it will decide everything."

There is a difference between Christian action motivated by moralism – by a "should" or "must" or even a solid reason, and Christian action flowing more from a real, personal relationship of love. Pope Benedict XVI was clear on this.

Moral exhortation certainly has its place; there is no denying that fact. Living up to moral and ethical standards and using our God-given brains is obviously part of making an integral, human response to God's unending, loving outreach to us. All of this is well and good, but it is not enough. We need love – the sacrificial love or *agape* – the mystery of the cross.

Saint Paul would put it this way:

> "The love of Christ urges us on...."[22]

---

[22] 2 Corinthians 5:14

TO BE CALLED IS TO BE SENT

There is a popular saying in Kiswahili that is translated: "To be called is to be sent." This Kenyan saying is used in instructing newly baptized adult Christians but applies to all of us.

The Church is missionary in its origin and nature. The Church is missionary by its very nature because its founder, Jesus Christ, was the first missionary. Saint Vincent de Paul called Jesus "the first missionary of the Father."

We are missionaries by reason of our baptism and confirmation.

Jesus gave us the mandate before he ascended into heaven:

> "Go therefore and make disciples of all nations, baptizing them in the name of the Father and of the Son and of the Holy Spirit, and teaching them to obey everything that I have commanded you. And remember, I am with you always, to the end of the age."[23]

To be called is to be sent.

That is us!

---

[23] Matthew 28:19-20

MY LIFE, MY MESSAGE

Bill Gates, Sr. wrote a book called *Showing Up for Life*. I have read it. There is a chapter entitled: "Making Your Life Your Message."

Mahatma Gandhi used to say this of himself: "My life is my message."

What about us? Is our life our message? We live our message by and through our vocation: married, single, widowed, religious, or ordained.

Gandhi often challenged Christian missionaries to observe the "apostolate of the rose." But the apostolate of the rose is applicable to every Christian, not just to missionaries in foreign lands.

A rose does not preach. It simply is. It simply radiates its fragrance and attracts us to it by its irresistible beauty. We used to have roses three times a year in Kenya. They were large, gorgeous, and multi-colored. I was particularly fond of the white and scarlet colors. Often, I would just stare at their beauty.

The most important thing is not the gospel we preach, but the life we live. This is how the early Christians evangelized. Their Gentile neighbors used to say:

"See how these Christians love one another."[24]

The Jesus Christ who the Gentiles and Jews recognized and accepted was the Jesus Christ lived out in each Christian life. Their lives were their message.

To paraphrase a thought of Saint Jean-Marie Vianney:

"When our hands have touched spices, they give fragrance to all they handle. Let us make our lives pass through the hands of Jesus. He will make them fragrant."

Did you ever get some Chrism oil on your hands? Now that is a sacred fragrance better than any cologne or perfume!

---

[24] Tertullian: CSEL, 69; Glover translation, Loeb edition

JOY

When we were novices, we lived in cubicles. Each of us had a bed, sink, desk, and a window, separated from each other by what we called curtains – three separate pieces of white canvas-type material that we pulled close when we retired for the night and gave us some privacy. I say "some" privacy because the curtains did not reach the ground and were the only things that prevented us from seeing others, but we could still hear all human noises!

Every morning, at five o'clock, the Care of Seminary walked past each cubicle, and said "Benedicamus Domino" (*Let us bless the Lord*). The Care of Seminary was our alarm clock; and our response – "Deo gracias" (*Thanks be to God*) meant that we were awake and would get out of bed. Incidentally, I held this job for six months.

This reminds me of Chesterton's jingle:

> "Wherever a Catholic sun doth shine,
> There's plenty of laughter and good red wine.
> God grant that it be ever so,
> Benedicamus Domino!"

Two of my favorite French authors are Paul Claudel and Leon Bloy. Father Leo Ebisch, C.M. would share with us quotations from these Catholic writers from a French publication he received every month. Ever since those college days, I have taken a genuine interest in the lives and writings of Claudel and Bloy.

Leon Bloy writes:

> "Joy is the most infallible sign of the presence of God."

Is that true – the most infallible sign?
Saint Paul tells us to live by the Spirit:

> "For what the flesh desires is opposed to the Spirit, and
> what the Spirit desires is opposed to the flesh; for these

are opposed to each other, to prevent you from doing what you want."[25]

"The fruit of the Spirit is love, joy, peace, patience, kindness, generosity, faithfulness, gentleness, and self-control.
If we live by the Spirit, let us also be guided by the Spirit."[26]

Saint Paul puts joy as the second in the list: The fruit of the Spirit is…joy.

Is this why Bloy says that joy is the most infallible sign of the presence of God?

When I delve into Bloy's life, I see that he has made an impression on some other well-known authors. Graham Greene, Jorge Luis Borges, Alejo Carpentier, and John Irving all have quoted Bloy in their writings. But I doubt if it was because of joy.

Bloy's life was anything but joyful. He acquired the nickname, "the ungrateful beggar." Perhaps, because of the turmoil in his life, Bloy came to see through the Spirit that joy was the most infallible sign of the presence of God.

What about us? Do we believe Bloy? Do we believe Saint Paul?

---

[25] Galatians 5:16-17
[26] Ibid., 5:22-25

JESUS

I remember several times in Kenya and Nigeria the little kids coming up to me and touching my skin. They would not say anything, just touch me.

Why was it white? What happened to it? One old tale was that there had been a mistake in nature, and some people ended up with no color, just white skin.

A British missionary lived alone, a single white man, among the African people, in a remote area of Tanzania. One day a British government official arrived on tour of the area. As is the tradition, great hospitality was shown the man. The children entertained the visitor with singing and dancing. After the official had left, some of the children went to their priest all excited...

"We saw a white man! We saw a white man!"

Several of the children said that their visitor was the first foreigner that they had ever seen. The priest was almost speechless. He said, "But I am a white man. I am a foreigner. I have been living with you for years."

One of the children immediately replied:

"You are not a white man; you are Jesus".

How did that missionary feel? Out of the mouths of babes comes incredible truth.

"You are Jesus." Could anyone ever say that about us? Yet, is that not our goal as Christians: to become more like Jesus?

Saint Paul says in Romans:

"Put on the Lord Jesus Christ."[27]

"It is no longer I who live, but it is Christ who lives in me. And the life I now live in the flesh, I live by faith in the Son of God, who loved me and gave himself for me."[28]

---

[27] Romans 13:14
[28] Galatians 2:20

SEEKERS

I think TV shows like *America's Got Talent*, *Britain's Got Talent*, and *Australia's Got Talent* are seekers; they seek talent, men and women who have a dream. The contestants are men and women who want to be found; they believe that they have what it takes to have their dream become a reality. We now have artists like Carrie Underwood, Susan Boyle, Paul Potts, and Mark Vincent, to name but four, among others.

There are seekers searching for something called talent, which exists in someone. People have talent, not things.

All of us are seekers. All of us want to find and be found.

Let us look at another level of seeking. There is a reading from Saint Anselm's *Proslogion* that I particularly like. I have used it for retreats and I have read it for my own reflection during the year. It still draws me.

> "Insignificant man, escape from your everyday business
> for a short while, hide for a moment from your restless
> thoughts.
> Break off from your cares and troubles and be less con-
> cerned about your tasks and labors. Make a little time
> for God and rest a while in him."

All of us – insignificant men and women as we are – need to do this whether it is a retreat, a day of recollection, a block of time set aside – whatever. Perhaps we need all the above examples for maintaining and deepening our relationship with God.

The reading from Saint Anselm concludes:

> "Teach me to seek you,
> when I seek you show yourself to me,
> for I cannot seek you unless you teach me,
> nor can I find you unless you show yourself to me.

Let me seek you in desiring you and desire you in seeking you,
find you in loving you and love you in finding you."[29]

Let us be seekers – always!
May this prayer be ours today!

[29] Cap.1: Opera omnia, Edit. Schmittm Seccovn, 1938, 1, 97-100

DO NOT JUDGE A BOOK BY ITS COVER

I met a most interesting French Vincentian priest, Pere Francois Brillet, C.M. in Yaounde, Cameroon. He has been a missionary in Africa, I would estimate since ordination, over 50 years ago.

As he told the story to me, his superiors in Paris sent him to the missions in Africa because they judged that he was not smart enough to teach in seminaries. The man since has held leadership positions in several countries for bishops. He has accomplished much in his long priestly life and ministry, and now is involved in priestly formation.

I am not certain how many languages he speaks, but it could be nine. He told me that after French, he thinks that his next best language was Amharic, then Arabic. From his mastery of English, I would never think his best language after French was Amharic. When we first met, he told me that he was so happy to see an American there because he could practice his American English rather than British English.

Do not judge a book by its cover.

Look at Jesus' selection of the twelve apostles. Be honest. Would you have chosen those men? They included 4 fishermen (two sets of brothers), a tax collector of questionable character, a man who probably was watched by the Roman military occupation forces because of his political views, and a few others about whom we really don't have enough information for any kind of critical judgment.

Not my choices, but they were Jesus' selection for the foundation of his church. And when one of them betrayed Jesus, he was replaced with another who was chosen by the early church membership. Afterward, the ascended Jesus chose a man by the name of Saul of Tarsus, who was a first-class persecutor of the first Christians.

From what tradition tells us, each of these men died a martyr's death for the church except Saint John, the Evangelist, the beloved disciple. Perhaps, because he had proved his love for God: he stood at the foot of the cross and perhaps more importantly, Jesus selected him to watch out for his Mother.

How fast are we in judging people? Isn't it an occupational disease for all of us? Yes, it is necessary to make judgment calls at times, but must we judge everyone's motives or moral character without sufficient knowledge?

How many book covers have we judged today?

THE ROSARY

What did I read some time ago? Teens are forbidden to wear the rosary around their necks during school hours. It is a religious item, and therefore prohibited. Is it a religious article or just "jewelry" for too many of them?

The rosary is "a veritable school of the Christian life," "the breviary of the common people," and "a compendium of the entire gospel."

When we pray the rosary, we are praying the gospel, and when we pray the gospel, we are praying Jesus Christ.

In reciting the rosary, we are, in fact, in contact with two of the most basic prayers in our Christian tradition: The Lord's Prayer and the Angelic Salutation. The third prayer is the "Glory be."

With the rosary, we sit at the feet of Mary and are led to contemplate the beauty on the face of Jesus and to experience the depth of his love. Any devotion of Mary leads us to Jesus. She is our teacher. What we find out is that not only does Jesus love us unconditionally, but so does his Mother.

In praying the rosary, the mysteries of Jesus' life and Mary's life interweave with the events of our lives. Not all mysteries are supernatural. Our lives are full of mystery. Reflecting on the mysteries in the life of Jesus and his Mother can help us understand the mysteries in our own lives.

We Christians are accustomed to think of our life patterns in terms of the paschal mystery – life, death, and resurrection – but, I think in that framework of the paschal mystery, we may well think of life-patterns as joyful, sorrowful, luminous, and glorious. Is not our earthy life made of those mysteries? Those mysteries in the lives of Jesus and Mary may help us in the comparisons and reflections of our lives.

KING JESUS, MIGUEL, AND CEFERINO

We Americans are fascinated with royalty as is evidenced by our interest in the royalty of Great Britain, but other kingdoms as well. Monarchs and queens grab our attention.

It is difficult for many to get a wrap on Jesus as king. They can understand him as Savior of humankind, as the Son of Man, as the Son of God, but king is something else. Yet what do we hear Jesus say to Pilate's question?

> "So you are a king?
> You say that I am a king."[30]

King Jesus moves his throne to the cross, and from the cross to the right hand of the Father.

A question to ask ourselves: Who sits on the thrones of our hearts? Is it King Jesus or is it greed, lust, or something else? Narcissism is alive and well in today's culture.

Here are two men who loved King Jesus.

Miguel Pro and other Jesuit novices were forced to flee to the United States from Mexico for safety. From Los Gatos, California they went to Granada, Spain. Because of Miguel's background with miners in Mexico and his ability to relate with them, he was sent to Belgium to study the Catholic labor movement. He was ordained a priest there August 31, 1925. His first assignment was ministry to the Belgium miners.

Because of health problems, Miguel returned to Mexico in 1926. The anti-Catholic government made priestly ministry very difficult. Any Catholic priest who celebrated the Eucharist or any sacrament risked arrest, torture, and even death.

Miguel and his brother, Roberto, were arrested under the pretext of their involvement in a plot to assassinate the former president of Mexico.

---

[30] John 18:39

Even though authorities knew both men were innocent, the two brother priests were condemned to death without benefit of due process or trial.

On November 27, 1927, in spite of a man shouting that he had a stay of execution for the two brothers, Miguel was brought before the firing squad.

He refused a blindfold, asked to pray, and with arms stretched out in form of a cross, shouted in a loud voice: "Viva Cristo Rey" (*Long live Christ the King*).

Ceferino Gimenez Malla was a married Spanish gypsy and an active member of the Society of Saint Vincent de Paul. Ceferino was imprisoned during the Spanish Civil War for protesting the arrest of a priest by the revolutionary militia. While in prison, Ceferino recited the rosary which totally angered his jailers. Believe it or not, he was offered his freedom if he would stop saying the rosary! He refused, because he considered devotion to the Blessed Virgin Mary a matter of great honor; he would not – could not – deny the Mother of God.

On August 2, 1936, he was killed by a firing squad, clutching his rosary and shouting, "Viva Cristo Rey!"

Both these men have been beatified by the Church. The Mexican Jesuit priest and the married Spanish gypsy horse trader. Although thousands of miles apart, they had much in common: their faith and their love for their sovereign, King Jesus.

JESUS AND MARY

Jesus is a master of disguises.

Mary is a master of adaptability.

Jesus, the master of disguises, comes to us identified in persons who are hungry, thirsty, imprisoned, sick, and homeless. He comes under the appearances of bread and wine. He comes to us through the reading and preaching of his Word. He comes to us under other sacramental signs. He comes when two or more are gathered in his name. He comes in the person of the priest. It is really him!

How do you recognize Jesus? What disguises does he wear? Matthew 25:31-46 is a good place to start or re-start our hunt for Jesus.

Mary, the master of adaptability, comes to the ordinary or poor children or to the common person, even the illiterate. She comes because Jesus appointed her our spiritual mother before his death on the wood of the cross.

Mary comes to fulfill her motherhood with her children. Mary lost one Son but gained the human race.

Mary is the woman of a thousand faces. She dresses in native outfits; her complexion takes on various shades and hues; she speaks particular dialects; she stands or floats in mid-air or sits. She is surrounded with dazzling light or by ovals and significant words. She sometimes holds things in her hands to make a point.

She comes as Prompt Succor, the Baker Woman, the Star of Hope, the Mystical Rose, the Undoer of Knots, the Virgin Mother of Tenderness, Our Lady of Ephesus, the Star of Evangelization. In recent times, Health of the Sick.

How do Jesus and Mary come to you?

How do they look?

MOTHER MARY

I gave two presentations on the Mother of Jesus to the collegiate seminarians in a day of recollection in Dallas when I was spiritual director.

I started off the second talk with two scenarios. They evolved around the place that Mary held during Jesus public ministry. I created the first scenario from my own imagination. The second scenario I also created from my imagination, but substantiated by the writings of Saint Maximus the Confessor who died in 662 AD. Maximus has left us the first complete biography of Mary based on the insights of several reputable saintly scholars and resources now lost.

Here is one scenario...

> One afternoon when no one was around the house and the carpenter's shop, Jesus sat down by his mother who was laying out clothes to dry. There was a silence, but then Jesus spoke:

> "Mother, it is time. I plan on leaving in two days to begin my mission. I know you were expecting this for some time. Could you put together a few things for me?"

> "I would like you to join me in a few months. But first I need to spend time in solitude and prayer. We can meet on the Sabbath at our synagogue the next full moon. Don't worry about the house and the shop. I will ask our relatives to take care of them."

> "What do you want me to do, Son?"

> "I intend to call other men to join me on my Father's mission. I foresee some women as well joining me as followers and taking care of our arrangements and daily needs, especially when we will be traveling from place to place.

I would like you to accompany us and oversee the women. Your presence and person would be invaluable to me and to those I will select and who will join me."

How do you see Mary in the life of Jesus? Did he leave her at home when he began his public ministry? Or did he take her with him?

Saint Maximus says that many women followed Jesus as disciples, as the gospels confirm. They were significant and influential members of Jesus' followers, "missionaries of love" as someone has called them. The "holy Mother of the Lord" guided and advised these women, acting as their mediator with her Son.

Plausible? Possible?

"Mary is our only savior from an abstract Christ."[31]

---

[31] Coventry Patmore, poet of the 19th century

WHAT TRUMPS SCIENCE?

A braggadocios French university student boarded a train in France and sat down next to an older man who seemed quite ordinary. The brash student noticed that the older gentleman was slipping beads through his fingers. He was saying the rosary.

"Sir, do you still believe in such outdated things?"
"Yes, I do; don't you?"

The student laughed.
"I don't believe in such silly things. Take my advice and throw that rosary out the window. Learn what science has to say about things."

"Science? I don't understand this science. Perhaps you can explain it to me, the man said softly, tears welling up in his eyes."

The student noticed that the man was deeply moved, and he did have some sensitivity; he didn't want to hurt the man's feelings any more than he had.

"Please give me your name and address, and I will send you some literature which might explain science to you."

The old man had some trouble retrieving his business card out of his jacket packet. He handed the card to the student who read the card and then hung his head in shame. The card read:

"Louis Pasteur, Director of the Institute of Scientific Research, Paris."

The young student had just encountered one of the greatest chemists and bacteriologists the world has ever known.
What trumps science?

QUEEN MOTHER

"The little unknown girl of Nazareth became the Queen of the World."[32]

Who would have thought that the young teenager from a small insignificant town would become Queen of Heaven and Earth? No other queen has ever held that title and could not. Yes, a woman could be a queen but only of restricted territory.

In the Old Testament monarchy, the queen of the Davidic Kingdom was the Queen Mother. Why? Because the kings had many wives, none of whom could be earmarked as queen. That honor was reserved for the mother of the king. She was Queen Mother.

We believe that Mary, the Mother of Jesus Christ, is Queen Mother. She reigns as spiritual mother of every human being with him in heaven, body, and soul. Her Son, the King of kings and Lord of lords, sits on his throne.

There is something uncharacteristic of this king and queen. They do not sit on their thrones all day doing nothing. They are with us.

Queen Mother Mary is carrying out the mission of mercy.

> "A great portent appeared in heaven: a woman clothed with the sun, with the moon under her feet, and on her head a crown of twelve stars. She was pregnant and was crying out in birth pangs, in the agony of giving birth."[33]

How many of you have been and are recipients of the Queen Mother's gifts?

Where do we sign in?

---

[32] Benedict XVI, August 22, 2010
[33] Revelation 12:1-6

HE MET JESUS IN PRISON

I heard Cardinal Van Thuan in Los Angeles at a convention about two years before he died. He gave a talk on Jesus. It was one of the best talks on Jesus that I have ever heard, and I have heard many as well as giving a few myself.

What was evident is that this was a man who truly not only knows Jesus but loves him.

The Communist government in Vietnam arrested Archbishop Francois Xavier on the Feast of the Assumption, 1975. He was imprisoned for 13 years, nine years of which were spent in solitary confinement. Two guards watched him day and night.

He never had a trial or a sentencing. For a long time, he could not pray because of his state of mind. Without the grace of God, he said he would have gone out of his mind.

Through the help of several guards, he was able to make a small cross out of wood which he hid in his soap. And he also was able to get a little wine…medicine for his stomach. He would say Mass from memory using his hand as the chalice using three drops of wine and one drop of water.

On the Feast of the Presentation of Our Lady, November 21, 1988, he was released from prison but confined to his house.

In God's providence, he ended up in Rome where Pope John Paul II gave him a Vatican position and named him a Cardinal.

Cardinal Francois Xavier told us in Los Angeles that he met Jesus in prison. Non-Christian prisoners often asked him, "Who is this Jesus?" "Why do you love him to the point of being willing to sacrifice your life for him in prison?"

The guards kept pressing him:

> "Does Jesus really exist? What is he like? Have you ever met him?"

Good questions for us?
What's Jesus like?
Have you ever met him?

CELIBACY

I know the standard lines:

"Celibacy without golf is irrelevant."

"Alcohol compensates for my celibacy."

The argument goes something like this:

I am celibate, which means that I cannot marry.
But it doesn't mean that I can't fool around.
(Translate this according to your own imagination.)

Celibacy means chaste celibacy. No marriage, no sex, heterosexual or homosexual.

Why does the Catholic Church continue to defend the practice of chaste celibacy that seems unnatural, unnecessary, and downright cruel? Why doesn't the Church get with it in the 21st century? Besides, would not marriage for clerics and religious greatly reduce sexual abuse?

There are a lot of reasons for chaste celibacy in the books, but I think the only one that makes sense is to speak of it in terms of the world to come.

The Sadducees confronted Jesus with their hypothetical example, which I am sure they thought was funny, ridiculous and impossible to answer, yet based on the Levirate Law of marriage.[34] Their test case: Who would be the husband of a woman in heaven who had married seven times but was childless? Jesus delved into deep theology which they never expected.

After this life on earth, there is not a replay of the same in heaven. Things will be different after we die. All relationships will be transformed. There is no marriage in heaven because there is no need for it. There is no sex in heaven.

---

[34] Luke 2): 27-38

Chaste celibacy is a sign of the world to come, which priests in the Latin Rite strive to live totally now as a disciple of Jesus Christ in imitation of Jesus who lived a life of chaste celibacy.

God chooses certain men and women to live as chaste celibates. It is not for everybody; it is not for anybody. These persons are to witness to a transcendent form of love, the way we will love in heaven.

Chaste celibacy is not easy in this world sex-saturated by commercials, TV sitcoms, reality shows, and movies. Pornography is available for everyone, married, single, and ordained.

Chaste celibacy is not getting any easier, but was it ever?

THE HITMAN'S ADVICE

I buy very few DVD's, but one I did buy was David Foster's first special on public television: *The Hitman*. I thoroughly enjoyed the program because of my love for music. It is great to be able to understand the lyrics of songs!

David Foster has written about 1000 songs, has had 100 hits, has won 15 Grammies, and is the writer and/or producer of many of the biggest names in the music industry.

I listened to an interview with Mr. Foster and was struck by several of the statements he made that are applicable to the spiritual life.

Mr. Foster said that he surrounded himself with successful people, not necessarily people in the music business. (The way the saints did it was to surround themselves with people like themselves: holy and wise.)

He said that the road to success is not curved. (Our salvation history and sin history is not curved either; they are linear.) "Innovation and creativity is the never-ending pursuit of something better – to improve the quality of our work and life."

Saint Vincent de Paul says that charity is inventive to infinity. There are no restrictions on inventiveness…the sky is the limit!

Good is the enemy of greatness. Being good is not good enough. You must do everything as best as it can be.

How many times have we heard?

> Good, better, best;
> never let it rest,
> until the good is better,
> and the better is best.

GUARDIAN ANGELS

If you live in New York City or San Francisco or Toronto or London or Tokyo or Cape Town, very likely you have known who the "Guardian Angels" are. They are and have been in other cities, large and small.

The Guardian Angels are a non-profit, international, volunteer organization of unarmed citizen crime patrollers. The organization was founded 13 February 1979, by Curtis Sliwa, originally to combat violence and crime on the New York City subways. The Guardian Angels patrol the streets and neighborhoods and provide education programs and workshops for schools and business through their chapters in 144 cities.

There are other Guardian Angels that many of us know...our own! We believe that every one of us has his or her own Guardian Angel. Saint Bernard of Clair Vaux said that Guardian Angels were proof...

> "That heaven denies us nothing that assists us and hence these celestial spirits have been placed at our sides to protect us, instruct us, and to guide us."[35]

One of the first prayers I ever learned was when I was perhaps three years old. Mrs. Lill Hall, whom I always called "Wee-Wee's Ma," taught me this prayer when we lived on North Avenue, east of Crawford (Pulaski), in Chicago.

> "Angel of God,
> My guardian dear,
> to whom his love commits me here,
> Ever this day,
> Be at my side, to light and guard, to rule and guide.
> Amen."

Saint Padre Pio used to tell his friends:

---

[35] Directory on Popular Piety and Liturgy, #216

"When you are in need of my prayer, address my Guardian Angel."

A bus load of pilgrims was on route to see Padre Pio when they were caught in a violent thunderstorm in the mountainous area. People were terrified. Someone on the bus remembered Padre Pio's words, and they prayed to his Guardian Angel. The bus made it safely.

The next day, at San Giovanni Rotondo, before the pilgrims had a chance to tell him about the storm, Padre Pio stopped them and smiled:

"Well, my children, last night you woke me up, and I prayed for you."

Where are we in our relationship with our Guardian Angel?

Do we ever pray to him or her? Especially, when we travel by plane or car, do we ever think of praying to our Guardian Angel for protection and a safe trip?

P.S. I pray to my Guardian Angel every day and always thank him/her for taking care of me.

SHOW YOUR POWER!

I remember seeing the pastor of Little Flower Church in Houston surrounded by a bunch of the grade-schoolers and leading the chant:

> "Little Flower, show your power!
> Little Flower, show your power!"

Saint Therese Martin, the Little Flower, the Carmelite saint, died when she was but 24 years old. Even though her death was at a young age what an impact she has had on people throughout the world including me!

A Vincentian confrere of mine, now deceased, Father Joe Gregor, said that in his country of Yugoslavia, there was a saying:

> "Never simplify anything you can complicate."

I dare say that we are faithful to doing that in church and state!

Saint Therese has simplified the spiritual life for us...do ordinary things in an extraordinary way out of love of God, with total dedication and child-like trust, ever ready to undertake any type of sacrifice.

That is pretty simple, but no one said that it was easy. But it is the shortcut through the pass.

Saint Therese said, before she died, that she would spend her heaven doing good things on earth. Let's take her up on that promise.

> "Little Flower, show your power!"

CHUTZPAH

Chutzpah comes from the Hebrew word meaning "audacity", "insolence", and "impertinence."

In Hebrew, chutzpah describes someone who has over-stepped the boundaries of accepted behavior, apparently without any shame. But, in Yiddish, chutzpah now can be used to express admiration for non-conformist behavior – gutsy audacity. We still say: "she has her gall to do that."

As Jesus said about Nathanael:

"Here is truly an Israelite in whom there is no deceit!"[36]

Or, as it is sometimes translated, "Here is truly an Israelite in whom there is no guile!"

Take Saint Catherine of Siena for example. During a time of great scandals in 14th century church, she wrote to a group of Cardinals in Rome:

"You are flowers that shed no perfume, but a stench that makes the whole world reek."

There is a good example of a holy woman's chutzpah!

Boundaries are significant in today's society. Too many people have over-stepped boundaries of accepted behavior apparently without shame, but not because of chutzpah for the good of others, but for the good of themselves. They have caused scandal, serious scandal, and have hurt many and have left victims outside the boundaries.

Dioceses and religious communities are conducting mandatory workshops for their employees and members on boundaries. Having clear boundaries is essential to a healthy personal and communal life.

---

[36] John 1:47

Go into any bookstore and you will find books on boundaries: boundaries in relationships, in marriage, in dating, with kids, at neighbors, and in the workplace.

We Christians must be alert, prudent, and cautious. Focusing so much on charity and being unselfish can get us into trouble because we forget our limits and overstep the boundaries of proper decorum, etiquette, and protocol.

NOTHING LEFT FOR YOURSELF

I often return to a breviary reading by Saint Charles Borromeo. I have used his remarks for others and for my own reflection.

Although the words were directed to his clergy, they are just as applicable for people in all walks of life.

> "Are you in charge of a parish?
> If so, do not neglect the parish of your own soul;
> do not give yourself to others so completely that you
> have nothing left for yourself.
> You have to be mindful of your people without becoming forgetful of yourself."[37]

These words are most fitting for today's pastor or parochial vicar or parish deacon or religious, especially in the situation of many places where a parish is equivalent to a conglomerate or where the priest has four or more missions spread out by miles and miles.

Running some parishes is like running small corporations. Meetings are held daily. Sports programs are going every night. There are church services going on several times a week, not counting, of course, funerals, marriages, quinceañeras, and multiple week-end masses.

Saint Charles' advice: do not neglect the parish of your own soul.

Are you in charge of a family? If so, do not neglect the life of your soul. Do not give yourself to the family members so completely that you have nothing left for yourself. Take care of yourself physically, spiritually, intellectually, emotionally....

This also applies to those in the single state where life is being lived in the express lane. The saint's words are worthy of one's reflection and action.

How many are afraid to see a doctor because they are paranoid that he or she may find something serious? How many people are afraid of dentists?

Take care of yourself!

---

[37] Acta Ecclesiae Mediolanensis Mediolani 1599, 177-1179

FIDELITY

The day our dad died of cancer in a suburbia hospital, I was pastor of Saint Vincent de Paul Church in Chicago. I had awakened early and felt the urgency to write. While he lay dying, I was reflecting on what our dad taught us. The questions I asked myself: What gift did he give us? What gift is he leaving us?

The answer came, without hesitation: fidelity. Our dad was a man of fidelity to God, to the church, to his children, grandchildren, friends, anyone he worked for, the Knights of Columbus, and even to his diseased wife, our mother.

I shared what I had written at his funeral. I got through it all, but almost lost it at the offertory procession when my nieces and nephews, his grandchildren, came up to the altar bearing lilies of the valley flowers – our mother's favorite flower, the official flower of our family.

We prove fidelity, not in the head or in the heart, but in action. Fidelity is sustained commitment. Fidelity is the gift that is needed today in our world: in families, churches, workplaces, relationships, etc.

I recently told a group of people that fidelity is one of the greatest gifts we can show: not to cave in when things get tough or to walk away because we feel disappointed that things didn't work out the way we wanted -- or walk away from someone or something because our feelings were hurt.

Stick with it. Perseverance.

Our Vincentian community used to make an annual eight-day retreat. The mediation for the morning of the day before the retreat was perseverance. We asked God that we might be able to stick with the resolutions and good purposes that we made during the eight days.

Too many of us are walking around with conditional clauses relative to our relationships, to God and to others. "I will stick with you, if...."

If "Semper fidelis" is good enough for our United States Marines, it seems to me to be good enough for every one of us: *Always faithful.*

WHAT HAS LOVE GOT TO DO WITH IT?

That's a good question.

I hear Tina Turner's song in my head: *What's love got to do with it?*

I remember seeing *Chorus Line* and hearing "Diana" singing the Edward Kleban and Marvin Hamlisch's song *What I did for love.*

I enjoy hearing Michael Ball, one of my favorite singers, sing: *Love Changes Everything* by Andrew Lloyd Webber and Don Black from *Aspects of Love.*

What's love got to do with it? Everything. I did it all for love. Love does change everything. Anything less than love is questionable and probably counterfeit.

Love changes everything: how you live and how you die; it does turn our world around. Love simplifies our motives and reduces them to one. The best proof of all of this: Jesus on the cross.

Saint Pope John Paul II wrote:

> "Man cannot live without love.
> He remains a being that is incomprehensible for himself,
> his life is meaningless, if love is not revealed to him,
> if he does not encounter love,
> if he does not experience it and make it his own,
> if he does not participate intimately in it."[38]

---

[38] Rememptor Hominis #10

THANKSGIVING DAY

My pleasant memories of Thanksgiving Day as a child were my mother's stuffing and our family's favorite desert, "Heavenly Hash." My mom would send me to the grocery store to buy "Silver Cup" bread. The stuffing had to be made from that brand and no other because, according to my mother, it held everything together better than any other.

Sometimes I helped with the preparation of it and the desert. "Heavenly Hash" consisted of quartered marshmallows, crushed pineapple, and real whipped cream. Of course, it had to be chilled.

My worse memory of Thanksgiving Day actually occurred the day after the holiday. I was coming down our street delivering the Chicago newspapers when I spotted a fire engine parked opposite our house in the middle of the street.

At that time, we had an old ice-box, and sometime after I had left to deliver papers, pneumonia gas started leaking. Because of its nature, the gas could have possibly killed my entire family. In God's providence, my sister Jeanne woke up and told our mother, who, in turn, woke all the others. My mother called the fire department. Several burly firemen picked up the icebox and placed it on our back porch.

We had much to be thankful for that holiday!

What are your fondest memories of Thanksgiving Day? Any not-so-good memories?

One of the former prolific spiritual writers was the Frenchman Father Raul Plus, S.J. One of his books has been republished: *The Rare Virtues*. I remember the book well from novitiate days.

The first rare virtue Father Plus mentions is *gratitude*. Although he wrote this book many years ago and classified gratitude as rare, how would he classify it now? What is rarer than rare?

Saint Vincent de Paul says that "ingratitude is the most heinous of crimes." Notice, Saint Vincent calls ingratitude a crime, not the opposite of virtue: a vice.

He says further:

"One of the most touching and edifying acts to be seen in the Church is gratitude. Nothing more completely wins the heart of God than gratitude. We should spend as much time in thanking God for his benefits as we spend in asking him for them."

Am I the only one or do others find people less polite today? Less people say "thank you" or "excuse me" or "pardon me."

Is one of the reasons for ingratitude "entitlement"?

Too many people think that they have everything coming to them; then no need to thank anyone.

BE READY TO RECEIVE

I had a wise and venerable spiritual director in Kenya. I learned much practical wisdom from the lips of Father Sidney, a Jesuit priest.

In one of our sessions, he mentioned that too many missionaries come to the missions with the idea in their heads that they are going to give the native people their wisdom and knowledge from their particular country and from their years of experience in priesthood or the religious life. And there is some truth to that, but these new missionaries are starting on the wrong foot. It is not what they are going to give Africa or Asia or the Solomon Islands; it's what these native people are going to give them.

What are these missionaries ready and willing to learn? What are they open to?

Are they ready to celebrate the Eucharist for two-to-three hours? Are they ready to have dancing and processions and singing?! It is not Kansas anymore!

Too many of us have closed down our in-take sources. We are so fixed, so closed, that it is difficult for us to receive. We would rather be givers.

> "No one sews a piece of un-shrunk cloth on an old cloak;
> otherwise, the patch pulls away from it, the new from the old,
> and a worse tear is made.
> And no one puts new wine into old wineskins,
> otherwise, the wine will burst the skins, and the wine is lost, and so are the skins;
> but one puts new wine into fresh wineskins."[39]

---

[39] Mark 2:21-22

LUST OR LOVE?

I love God.

I love Our Lady of the Miraculous Medal.

I love Saint Vincent de Paul and Blessed Frederic Ozanam.

I love my sisters and all my nieces and nephews and grandnieces and nephews.

I love the Chicago White Sox.

I love English toffee.

I love breaded pork tenderloin and French fries and creamed peas.

I love New York at Christmas.

In the English language, we use one love for love of persons and things, whereas in Greek there are distinctions. In the New Testament, we can only see these specifications in Greek.

Phileo: "brotherly love." We know Philadelphia. Phileo is a human response to something that we have experienced to be delightful.

Agape: charitable, selfless, altruistic, and unconditional love. It is the way God is seen to love humanity. It is the way that Christians strive to love one another.

Then the Greeks have two other verbs for love not used in the New Testament.

Eros: sexual love.

Storge: child-to-parent love.

> "For God so loved the world that he gave his only Son, so that everyone who believes in him may not perish but may have eternal life. Indeed, God did not send the Son into the world to condemn the world, but in order that the world might be saved through him."[40]

I highly recommend C.S. Lewis' book: *The Four Loves* for knowledge and reflection.

---

[40] John 3:16-17

Saint Augustine tells us that we should be able to know the difference between love and lust. As lust is one of the capital sins that plague humanity, it is important to know the difference. Considering his past life, Augustine knew the difference!

According to him, lust is overindulgence, but to love and be loved is what he has sought for his whole life. He often said, "I was in love with love."

Love of another human being often brings jealousy, suspicion, fear, anger, and contention.

To love God is "to attain the peace which is yours."

The cholera that is infecting humanity throughout the world is pornography. It is really a pandemic. It is done for lust. It is the ring in the nose for the married, single, widowed, and ordained. Pornography is a vicious habit that respects no one, that sucks you in, and refuses to let you go. It is among the worst of addictions.

WHERE AM I GOING?

I played a part in the musical comedy *Paint Your Wagon* by Alan J. Lerner and Frederic Lowe during my college years. One of the memorable songs was a cast number: *A Wanderin' Star...*

> "I was born under a wanderin' star.
> When I get to heaven
> Tie me to a tree
> Or I'll begin to roam
> And soon you know where I will be"

How many of us act as if we were born under a wanderin' star? I am not talking about the tinkers or people of that type, but those who move from one job to another, one relationship to another.

Jesus knew where he was going. He had a plan: to do his Father's will. He kept in touch with that will by his prayer. He spent blocks of time away from the apostles and disciples by himself in remote places. Before every major decision, he made time for prayer.

You and I are in the same boat. We seek God's will in our life.

The Magi followed a wandering star and found Jesus.

We do not need a star. We know where he is.

THERESE FOUND HER NICHE

Saint Therese of Lisieux was a Carmelite nun in a French monastery leading an ordinary life, but she was tormented. She had the unfulfilled desire for martyrdom. This torment included a barrage of distractions during her prayer.

What to do? She tells Sister Marie of the Sacred Heart in her *The Story of a Soul* (chapter XI) that she delved into Saint Paul's letters hoping to find alleviation to her quest.

Therese's eyes lighted up in Paul's First Letter to the Church in Corinth. Paul is very explicit: not everyone can be apostles, prophets, or teachers, etc. His words in Chapter 12 were well and good, but it didn't satisfy her the way she wanted.

She kept reading and found her consolation in Chapter 13. As Saint Paul says, she found the best way: "This more excellent way of going to God is charity."

Therese continues:

> "I couldn't see myself in any of the members mentioned by St. Paul; or rather I wanted to see myself in all of them.

> "Charity gave me the key to my vocation.
> The Church must have a heart -- this heart must be on fire with love. I saw that it was love alone which moved her other members, and that were his love to fail, apostles would no longer spread the gospel, and martyrs would refuse to shed their blood."

Therese says:

> "I saw that all vocations are summed up in love, and that love is all in all, embracing every time and place because it is eternal.

I have found my vocation and my vocation is love. I have discovered where it is that I belong in the Church – the niche God has appointed me."

Have we found our niche – or are we still looking for it? It is possible to find it in Sacred Scripture.

THE NON-MIRACLE SAINTS

Most of the saints or extraordinary persons that I am drawn to are the non-miracle workers. I say most because there are a few exceptions like Saint Martin de Porres. He was my hero since my teens. In fact, when I first got to know him and pray to him, he was not yet canonized. To me, he was Blessed Martin de Porres.

Later in my life, Saints Vincent de Paul, Louise de Marillac, John Gabriel Perboyre, Justin de Jacobis, Elizabeth Ann Seton, Blessed Rosalie Rendu and Frederic Ozanam took primary places in my personal litany of saints.

When I look at them in depth I see interesting facts. Not necessarily in any order: several had been married with children or missionaries or martyrs; most were French, and, above all, were founders or inspiration for the world-wide Vincentian Family.

But another thing is striking, and I see it in the life of Saint Vincent de Paul.

Saint Vincent is one of those saints who seem to disappear behind their multiple achievements, and the same can be said of the others in my litany. These people accomplished much good for others, especially for those in the poor and needy category.

We don't read of any spectacular miracle performed through the hands of Saint Vincent de Paul nor from the others on my list. They were people who fell in love with God and his poor. For Vincent, he also did much for priesthood and priests. He had a tremendous love for his vocation which manifested itself in his ministry of those with the same vocation. Vincent started retreats for ordinands, "Tuesday Conferences" for bishops and priests (continuing education and formation sessions), and he became vitally involved in the establishment of seminaries. He founded twenty seminaries.

When we try to seek the man or woman, we find too often what they accomplished. But no one is ever beatified or canonized in the Catholic Church because of their accomplishments, no matter how many or how extraordinary. People are canonized for holiness of life.

What was Saint Vincent's secret and the secret of those not martyred?

They heroically practiced the three theological virtues of faith, hope, and charity, and the four cardinal virtues of justice, prudence, fortitude, and temperance. For those in the Vincentian Family, this would include the five special virtues: simplicity, humility, mortification, meekness, and zeal for souls.

Their vocation and ministry were their means of holiness: their love for the poor and poverty, their love for the priest and priesthood, their love for God and humanity.

SUFFERING

Suffering – a mystery

> a fact of life
> my personal experience
> sources: external and internal: others-made and self-made

Mankind has been asking the question for thousands of years... Why? If there is a God, how could he allow it? God is always the fall-guy. I don't have the answers, but I do know the mystery and have seen suffering and experienced it in my own life as you have.

We believe it is not God-inflicted, but often human-inflicted.

Look at every continent, and what do we see? Somewhere, some place, human beings are violating the rights of others in grievous and malicious ways, often under the pretense of power, greed, and control.

> Suffering: man's inhumanity to man
> cruelty, torture, violence, crime, rape
> physical abuse, emotional abuse, sexual abuse,
> coronavirus...

What about man's inhumanity to Jesus, God-man? Scourging, crowning with thorns, ridicule, mockery, carrying a wooden beam weighing perhaps 200 pounds, dehydration, excessive blood loss, nails into his hands and feet, evolving cramps throughout the body, and as-phyxiation. How could God allow that? How could Jesus (God) allow that to himself? There had to be a higher reason!

One of my sisters would say to me when I was complaining about something bothering me:

> Offer it up!" And I would sometimes fire back: "You
> offer it up!
> But she was right, but how to offer it up?

We Christians believe in redemptive suffering. We believe that human suffering, when accepted and offered up in union with the Passion of Jesus, can remit the just punishment for one's sins or for the sins of another. I will never forget visiting a woman who was dying of bone cancer and looked more and more like an Auschwitz survivor. We would talk about her suffering. And one day she asked me if she could offer her suffering for me? I was overwhelmed! This woman was offering her suffering for my sins. What an act of charity! Redemptive suffering is, in the final analysis, charity. Acts of charity done in union with the Suffering Jesus.

Read the Book of Job.

Read or listen to Archibald MacLeish's play *JB*.

What about Philip Yancey's book: *Where is God When It Hurts?*

Will they give us answers? Give them a try.

OKAY, I GIVE UP: WHAT IS IT?

What is holiness? We hear it from pulpits; we read about it in books. Holiness is like spirituality…not easy to define. Our best bet is probably descriptions.

First, an important digression. Why holiness? Why all the talk about it? The main reason:

> The church calls each and every one of us to holiness because Jesus does.
>> "Be perfect, therefore, as your heavenly Father is perfect."[41]
> Saint Paul tells the Church of Thessalonica:
>> "For this is the will of God, your sanctification."[42]

In my younger days, I wasn't sure what holiness was. I knew the saints were holy people, and I had the misconception that priests, sisters, and brothers were holy by the very reason of their special calling. Of course, I found out that was wrong. I started to meet, and still do, married persons, single persons, widowers who make those of us ordained or consecrated look like minor leaguers hungering for a berth on a major league roster!

That is what holiness is: a quest. We are sojourners seeking to be who we were intended to be.

The church teaches that all followers of Jesus Christ – that is us – of whatever rank, status, or serial number – is called to the fullest of the Christian life and to the perfection of charity. There are no exceptions. Forget about the fine print.

One other thing: too many people have thrown in the towel on holiness because they have this screwy idea that holiness means sinlessness. I have never met any sinless human beings in my long life. I have met probably three identifiable holy persons, but they weren't sinless. Only

---

[41] Matthew 5:48
[42] 2 Thessalonians 4:3

Jesus Christ and his Mother were sinless. We are living in an imperfect world with imperfect people who do a lot of imperfect things.

Okay, but what is holiness?

We turn to Saint Vincent de Paul for a solid description:

> "Holiness consists in doing well the will of God. Who is the most holy? The one whose *will* is most in accord with the will of God. Holiness is uniting our will with God's will so that his and ours are really the same will."

"Put on the Lord Jesus Christ."[43]

---

[43] Romans 13:14

SPIRITUALITY

There are a ton of books on the market on the subject of spirituality. Go into any Christian or secular bookstore and there they are. In fact, the major stores have a sectional sign.

We can't forget that there are numerous spiritualities: Christian, Jewish, New Age, Hindu, Islam…the list is long. I am talking about spirituality for Catholics, but certainly applicable for others.

I read that trying to define spirituality is like trying to nail Jello to the wall.

The late Pope John Paul II has, in my mind, given the better descriptions of spirituality:

> "It is life in Jesus and in the Spirit that is accepted in faith, expressed in love and inspired by hope. By spirituality we mean not a part of life, but the whole of life guided by the Holy Spirit.
>
> In the past, and perhaps now, we have departmentalized our life into pigeon holes, and we name them: family, work, socializing, recreation, work-out, church, etc. We have divided ourselves into numerous parts. People talk about body and soul, or body, mind, and spirit. That type of thinking keeps us disunified."

Pope John Paul continues:

> "There cannot be two parallel lines in your existence: on the one hand, the spiritual life with its values and demands. And, on the other hand, the worldly life, that is, family life, work, study, relationships, the responsibilities of public life and in culture. Every activity, every situation, every duty are occasions so ordered

by God for a continuous exercise of faith, hope, and love."[44]

In other words, spirituality has to do with the whole of our life – with who we are and everything we do.

The church reminds us that this spirituality takes its particular character from the circumstances of our life: our age, our stage in life, our state of health, our social state. This makes a lot of sense and is so practical.

We are called to develop the qualities and talents given to us in accord with the conditions of our life, and we should use the gifts that we have received from God.[45]

And I would add...gifts to be used for others, especially those in need.

---

[44] Lay Members, # 59
[45] Apostolate of Laity, # 4

MORE SPIRITUALITY/HOLINESS

There is a scholastic adage which is applicable when speaking about spirituality and holiness: *agere sequitur esse* (to do follows to be).

To be comes first, then *to do.* Spirituality primarily has to do with who we are. It permeates and penetrates our entire being. Spirituality identifies a person: Catholic, Lutheran, Jesuit, Franciscan, Benedictine, Muslim, Hindu, etc. What we do does not define who we are although that is usually the first thing we ask. "Hello, I'm Kara Gomilla and I work for this department store." "Hi, I'm Kris Prangle and I'm an IT-tech. What do you do for a living?"

When speaking of spirituality, Pope John Paul II used to talk about unity of life.

No one is ever canonized in the Catholic Church because of achievements, scholarship, talents, or set-skills. No one is ever canonized in the Catholic Church because of international fame or reputation. The criteria are heroic virtues. That's the bottom line.

The way I see it, spirituality is a means to an end, and the end is holiness. Spirituality provides the way, the components, the spirit, and the means of growing in holiness. A person lives out spirituality in daily living as life unfolds day after day, year after year.

So we follow the spirituality of Saint Ignatius, Saint Francis of Assisi, Saint Benedict, Saint Vincent de Paul. These saints provide us with the materials, the means to acquire holiness like they did.

Can we become holy by not following any of those schools? Oh, yes! How? We follow the teaching of Jesus as read in his gospels and as taught by the church and lived out in one's vocation in life.

No one is born a saint. It takes blood, sweat, and tears in cooperation with God's grace to become holy.

There is a rule about antique jewelry: the back is as important as the front. The information on the back tells us about the place of origin, date of manufacture, its maker, its authenticity. Spirituality is the back side of holiness. People see the front side of us, the effects of our spirituality.

THE POOR:
ALWAYS AND FOREVER?

Jesus said it in the Gospel of Matthew:

> "For you always have the poor with you, but you will not
> always have me."[46]

This is quoted by two other evangelists: Mark and John.

Some people think that Jesus' words, *you always have the poor with you*, mean that fighting poverty is a waste of time, energy, and money and that it is a losing battle. And we will never win no matter what we do or how hard we fight.

Others think that this is the way God wants the world: he wants some poor and miserable people roaming the streets of every nation in every generation until he comes again, because, after all, Jesus did say that we will have poor with us now and always!

I find this kind of thinking deplorable to say the least.

Such ideas indicate a miscalculation of who Jesus is and what Jesus taught during his public ministry. Look at his public ministry: feeding thousands, healing the sick and mentally ill people, raising the dead, and other random acts of kindness.

As Father Thomas Merton wrote:

> "God is: mercy within mercy within mercy."

The poor are the sacraments of Christ: outward signs of his presence among us. What does Jesus say in Matthew 25:31-46? He identifies himself with the least of our brothers and sisters.

What does it say about our government?

If the poor must be with us always, let's do something about reducing the number, and we can do that by eliminating the root causes of poverty.

---

[46] Matthew 26:11

DIVINE PROVIDENCE

I have eliminated from thinking (well, I have greatly reduced) words like coincidence, chance, good or bad luck, and accident. What has taken their place is divine providence. It has always been in my spiritual vocabulary, but it has advanced to a higher rung in my spiritual life and in how I view spirituality in general.

It is important to remember that God speaks to us in multiple ways. A case in point…

> During a horrible flood, a man goes to the top of his roof. He prays and implores God to rescue him. Afterward, a helicopter comes but the man refuses their help; he doesn't need it. Soon after, a police boat comes, but the man refuses their help. The man becomes angry with God. "Why have you not saved me?
> And God answers: "I sent a helicopter and a boat for you and you turned them down."

Saints like Vincent de Paul saw God acting in their lives through persons, events, and situations as secondary causes. God manifested his will through urgent needs. God spoke through these secondary causes, whether men and women or happenings or pressing needs of the faithful, especially the poor.

At its root, devotion to divine providence is the deep conviction of the attentive presence of God who walks with us in the varied experiences of human existence that we know well: light and darkness, grace and sin, plan and disruption, peace and turmoil, health and sickness, life and death. We have to be alert to God's voice and action, be it a police boat or helicopter.

Father Thomas Merton, OCSO has left us a Providence Prayer:

> "My Lord God, I have no idea where I'm going.
> I do not see the road ahead of me, and I cannot know for certain where it will end.

Nor do I really know myself, and the fact
that I think I am doing your will does not mean I am
actually doing so.
But I believe the desire to please you does in fact
please you,
and I hope I have that desire in everything I'm doing.
I hope I will never do anything apart from that desire,
and I know if I do this you will lead me by the right road,
though I may know nothing about it.
Therefore, I will trust you always,
though I may seem to be lost and in the shadow of death.
I will not fear for you are ever with me,
and you will never leave me to face my perils alone."[47]

[47] "The Merton Prayer" from *Thoughts in Solitude, copyright 1956, 1958*

THE MORNING OFFERING

A lot of years ago, Jimmy Durante sang his song *Start Off Each Day with a Song*. He was suggesting to people if we start off each day with a song, we will feel better, we'll even look better, even when things go wrong.

Here is a better idea…start off each day with prayer!

I have seen prayer cards with "The Morning Offering" of the Apostolate of Prayer attached to many mirrors on medicine cabinets in rectories throughout the United States. Whether it be in a guest room or in a room occupied by a priest, there it is. And it is a good place to have the prayer, because it is one of the first things a person sees in the morning and frequently during the day.

> "O Jesus,
> through the Immaculate Heart of Mary,
> I offer you my prayers, works, joys and sufferings
> of this day for all the intentions of your Sacred Heart,
> in union with the Holy Sacrifice of the Mass
> throughout the world,
> in reparation for my sins,
> for the intentions of all my relatives and friends,
> and in particular for the intentions of the Holy Father.
> Amen."

Yes, there are other versions of The Morning Offering. Some people use their own words which is fine. The whole idea is to kick-start our day with prayer and offer that day with all that it may bring to God.

VERNACULAR SPIRITUALITY

Archbishop Fulton Sheen used the term "vernacular spirituality" in a talk he gave at the National Convention of the Society of Saint Vincent de Paul many years ago.

Why did he use that term? What does it mean?

I can't give any definitive commentary on Archbishop Sheen's comments, but I think that he was referring to the ordinary tasks and responsibilities of everyday life. Vernacular spirituality is within the reach of everyone. It is finding the sacred in the ordinary and God in everyday life.

Holiness does not need extraordinary phenomena like bi-location, levitation, apparitions, voices, whatever, to be authentic. Our search for the sacred will lead through the mundane.

Saint Vincent de Paul said that God attends to the affairs of our souls, while we are attending to those of our vocation. Vincent's mandate always was "love of God is exercised by the strength of our arms and the sweat of our brows."

Sometimes we think that we need to be engrossed in major projects. Saint Vincent de Paul says that little actions done to please God are not subject to vanity as other actions that are more brilliant, which often go up in smoke. And he adds: "Be attentive to the smallest circumstances, in order that nothing may be wanting in what we do."

The practical question for all of us: okay, we agree with the concept of vernacular spirituality, but how does it play out? How do I maintain and sustain this spirituality in my life?

I propose two suggestions again from my inspiration, Saint Vincent de Paul:

> Human actions become actions of God when they are performed in him and through him.[48]

---

[48] Correspondence, Conferences, Documents, Vol XII, p.152, 28 March 1659

> We must sanctify our occupations by seeking God in
> them and by doing them rather than to get them done.[49]

Both these suggestions, these ways, take effort on our part. We need to build a habit.

But, in the long run, we will notice a radical change in our vernacular spirituality.

---

[49] Idem, Vol XII, p.112, 21 February 1859

EGOS

Can you have a big ego and still be humble? Is it possible?

John the Baptist had a giant ego, but yet is known for his humility. We hear that ego when he describes himself as:

> "The voice of one crying in the wilderness: 'Prepare the way of the Lord'...
> You brood of vipers!"

To the crowds:

> "Whoever has two coats must share with anyone who has none; and whoever has food must do likewise."

To the tax collectors:

> "Collect no more than the amount prescribed for you."

To the soldiers:

> "Do not exhort money from anyone by threats or false accusation and be satisfied with your wages."[50]

John says of Jesus:

> "I am not worthy to untie the thong of his sandal."[51]

Look at Saint Jerome. He was a brilliant scripture scholar and writer, but had a big ego plus a mouth to go with it. Many saints are remembered for some extraordinary virtue in their lives, but Saint Jerome is frequently remembered for his bad disposition. No one ever doubted what he thought: he called a spade a spade.

---

[50] Luke 3:4, 7, 10-14
[51] John 1:27

What about other saints? Did they have big egos? Do saints need big egos?

Take Saint Vincent de Paul. He is known for his meekness or gentleness, but remember he had to deal with two Prime Ministers of France, who happened to be, first, Cardinal Armand Richelieu and then Cardinal Jules Mazarin. These two had egos the size of Monte Blanc. It was Vincent's ego against Richelieu and Mazarin's egos.

How about Saint Frances Xavier Cabrini? I heard stories about her ego. She probably needed a big ego dealing with some of the big hierarchical egos she faced in her ministry with Italian immigrants.

I dare to say that if I portray a big ego most of you would call me conceited or madly in love with myself or other pejorative terms.

I think that saints had big egos to stand before the world and speak what they believed to be the truth and nothing but the truth. I include people like Blessed Teresa of Calcutta and Blessed Pope Pius IX, and Blessed Pope John XXIII. I think the late Pope Benedict XVI had a big ego for the same reason.

You can have a big ego and not be an egoist. Egoists are full of themselves (you know some, I presume), but a big ego can be full of God. Ego and humility are not contradictory terms. You can have one and the other.

We used to talk about persons with strong inner authority. What did that mean? I think that it often meant people with strong egos; people who felt security inside with the gifts given them by God – powerful self-images. I once heard an archbishop say in the course of a conversation that we once had a good number of pastors like that, but they are few and far between in today's church.

Perhaps the problem today is not humility but weak egos?

SIN

Whatever happened to sin?

Absolutely nothing! Not only is it well and alive, but stronger than ever. Sin exists but too few know it – in their very selves.

I remember well the flack that Doctor Karl Menninger's book caused: *Whatever Happened to sin?*

And I remember the words of Pope Pius XII:

"The sin of the century is the loss of the sense of sin."[52]

Do you think that Pope Pius XII would say the same about this century?

Robert Louis Stevenson's novella, *The Strange Case of Dr. Jekyll and Mr. Hyde,* tells us the story of a brilliant scientist who thinks that the evil side of the human condition can be eradicated through chemicals, and if so, then only good will prevail in our world. The thought is more than utopian! Doctor Jekyll tries and tries various formulas. When he is refused assistance by the medical profession, he begins injecting himself with the chemicals. The results are devastating. Doctor Jekyll becomes Mister Hyde, one evil person. It is a case of *reverse conversion.* Chemicals do not take away sin.

Father Eugene Maly, a scripture scholar, whom I met and admired, wrote a book before he died called *Sin: Biblical Perspectives.* Father Gene talks about one of the phrases used in the New Testament for sin: "missing the mark" (*hamartia* in Greek).

When we sin, we miss the mark.

When the archer draws his bow, but the arrow falls short of its target, he missed the bull's eye. When we sin, we miss the required standard of what is right.

Saint Paul says:

---

[52] 26 October 1946

"Since all have sinned and fall short of the glory of God."[53]

The one common denominator that transcends all race, religion, gender, sexual orientation, and financial status is sin; we don't need to forget it because we can't.

Sin is alive and well in the 21st century!

Just ask somebody. You know my personal answer.

---

[53] Romans 3:23

ADVENT

Let's start in the very beginning; it's a very good place to start.

The church begins its liturgical year with the First Sunday of Advent.

It is tough today to celebrate the four Sundays of Advent because of what's happening all around us. We are seeing Christmas commercials on television and Christmas decorations in stores and in our malls weeks before Thanksgiving. The merchants are cranking up for the holiday sales while displaying Halloween items!

What to do about it? What *can* we do about it? It is difficult to try to pretend that Christmas isn't upon us, and yet we want to get into the spirituality of Advent. The Advent wreath helps. So does the Advent calendars and the Advent readings for the daily Masses. I find these readings and those in the Office of Readings in the breviary to be some of the most beautiful and thought-provoking. Some families have their own traditions to strive to focus on Advent while the Christmas frenzy is whirling around our heads.

The word "Advent" means "coming."

Advent is about three comings of Jesus. Saint Bernard delivered an excellent talk to his fellow monks on the three comings. I would like to earmark the three as *history, mystery,* and *majesty.*

> *Our Lord comes in history.* He has come. We say at mass: "Christ has died; Christ has risen; Christ will come again."

> Jesus came as a new-born baby at Bethlehem. When we celebrate Christmas, we are celebrating "Christ-mas."

> Advent is a time to renew our faith in the baby Jesus whose birth we hail as the long-awaited Savior – our personal Savior, who can save us.

> *Our Lord comes in mystery.* He comes to us in word, sacrament, grace, and mercy.

Jesus is reborn in our daily lives in hundreds of ways. Our task is to recognize him with eyes of faith.

Our Lord comes to us in majesty. He will come in glory. As the priest prays after the Our Father at Mass: "as we wait in joyful hope for the coming of our Savior, Jesus Christ."

We wait during Advent for the historical Jesus who enters our time zone. He comes and pitches his tent among us.

Our mantra for Advent is: "Maranatha! Come, Lord Jesus!"

THE DEVIL

Years ago, one of my wisdom persons, Ruth, gave me her copy of C.S. Lewis' *The Screwtape Letters* as a gift. That gift came alive again when I saw the theatrical production in New York City. I thoroughly enjoyed it!

Is it just good theatre? Is it a fairy tale? Is it a myth that Christianity keeps perpetuating for some perverse reasons?

The answer to all the above questions is NO. Like sin, the devil is alive and well and working in our neck of the woods – in fact, doing a number on each one of us.

The Screwtape Letters is a series of letters from a devil named Screwtape to his nephew, Wormwood, about how to win a Christian away from God, whom Screwtape calls "The Enemy." Toadpipe is Screwtape's scribe.

In sacred scripture, the devil has many names, the better known are: the accuser, the adversary, the antichrist, Beelzebub, Satan, great red dragon, Lucifer, murderer, prince of this world, serpent, son of perdition, tempter, thief, and wicked one.

Perhaps some of you have your own names for the devil that we can't print.

One of the devil's greatest ploys is to get us not to believe in his existence. The great deceiver loves that. Then he's got us.

I have seen evil; so have you. I have seen evil perpetrated by individuals who wanted power and any means was permissible, including murder, rape, destruction of property, and theft. They produce fear among people, minimize their capability to retaliate, decimate families, and neighborhoods.

I have seen people with some means instantly made poor, and the poor made poorer.

Is there no evil in the world? Look around you. Look at the headlines and listen to the news casts.

We call evil personified Satan, and sometimes Satan comes to us in human form.

The deceased comedian, Flip Wilson, did an impersonation of a young woman: Geraldine. He gave the world Geraldine and the catch phrase: "The devil made me to do it!"

How many of us say that phrase or, if we don't say it, think it?

The devil made me do it!

RE-NEW

There is a psalm-prayer in the breviary (Monday, Morning Prayer, Week III) that I particularly like, and I find thought provoking:

> "Lord, you have renewed the face of the earth.
> Your Church throughout the world sings you a new song,
> announcing your wonders to all.
> Through a virgin, you have brought forth a new birth in our world;
> through your miracles, a new power,
> through your suffering, a new patience,
> in your resurrection, a new hope,
> and in your ascension, a new ministry."

Renewal is a slow process. The best proof I know is to look in the bathroom mirror. I am a work in progress, and the progress moves too often at a snail's pace.

The call of Jesus is for renewal.

Jesus came to Galilee, proclaiming the good news of God, and saying:

> "The time is fulfilled, and the kingdom of God has come near; repent and believe in the good news."[54]

Saint Paul reiterates more than once:

> "So if anyone is in Christ, there is a new creation: everything old has passed away; see everything has become new!"[55]

> "You were taught to put away your former way of life, your old self, corrupt and deluded by its lusts, and to

---

[54] Mark 1:14-15
[55] 2 Corinthians 5:17

be renewed in the spirit of your minds, and to clothe yourselves with the new self, created according to the likeness of God in true righteousness and holiness."[56]

"Seeing that you have stripped off the old self with its practices and have clothed yourselves with the new self, which is being renewed in knowledge according to the image of its creator."[57]

Renewal is 24/7, 52 weeks a year. It is not only a Lenten practice or as a result of an annual retreat. The ball is in our court.

---

[56] Ephesians 4:20-24
[57] Colossians 3:10

PRAYER FOR PEACE

We owe Saint Francis of Assisi a great deal of gratitude for this prayer. It is a favorite of thousands of people, Christian and non-Christian alike:

> Lord, make me an instrument of your peace,
> where there is hatred, let me sow love;
> where there is injury, pardon;
> where there is doubt, faith;
> where there is despair, hope;
> where there is darkness, light;
> where there is sadness, joy;
>
> O Divine Master, grant that I
> may not so much seek to
> be consoled as to console;
> to be understood as to understand;
> to be loved as to love.
>
> For it is in giving that we receive;
> it is in pardoning that we are pardoned;
> and it is in dying that we are born to eternal life. Amen.

THE MISSIONER'S PRAYER

The Missioner's Prayer is a favorite prayer of many in the Vincentian Family and used extensively by Vincentian priests engaged in parish missions. We said it daily in Kenya.

The prayer is attributed to the French missionary martyred in China for the faith, Saint John Gabriel Perboyre, C.M. This is an English version:

> O my Divine Savior, transform me into yourself.
> May my hands be the hands of Jesus,
> May my tongue be the tongue of Jesus.
>
> Grant that every faculty of my body
> may serve only to glorify you.
>
> Above all, transform my soul and its powers,
> that my memory, my will and my affections may be the memory,
> the will and the affections of Jesus.
> I pray you to destroy in me all that is not of you.
>
> Grant that I may live but in you and by you and for you,
> and that I may truly say with Saint Paul,
> "I live now, not I, but Christ lives in me."

MARRIAGE

I received a letter from a very close friend of mine, a married man, in the middle of the Desert War. He wrote, "Celibacy sucks!" He talked about how much he missed his wife and children.

Is marriage a roller coaster ride? Some think marriage is not for keeps, even good ones. Some think that it is better to cohabitate but not get married. They say "a marriage license is only a piece of paper." Some are afraid of marriage because they experienced their parent's failing marriage and wanted no part of that. Some see the figures: over 50% of marriages end in divorce and don't want to go through that horrific pain, especially if children are involved. Some hold that marriage should be legalized between same sex couples. And the list goes on.

Unfortunately, the Catholic Church is getting to be like the Lone Ranger; it has definite teachings on marriage. Here are a few of them.

Marriage is a lifelong commitment and covenant of love pledged between a man and a woman. In marrying, they promise that with the help of God's grace they will love one another faithfully and fruitfully, with an exclusive and uncompromised love. Which means, among other things, that the possibility of the creation of new human life must be kept open, in accord with the first command God gave human beings "be fertile and multiply."[58]

Marriage is a sacrament. A sacrament is *a visible sign instituted by Christ to impart sanctifying grace.* The sign of the sacrament of marriage is the exchange of consent and vows by the couple. But the marriage itself is in a real sense also a sacrament, whose sign is the love pledged on the wedding day and lived out in the circumstances of life. This love is a visible sign of Christ's unconditional, sacrificial, unending, and fruitful love for the church. Husbands and wives are called to be living witnesses to the reality and presence of Christ's love for his bride, the church.

Marriage is for life. The reason is because permanency is intrinsic not only to its nature, but also to faithfulness to the sacramental sign of

---

[58] Genesis 1:28

spousal love. A sacramental marriage is a living model of Christ's love for the church.

I recommend Bishop Kevin W. Vann's booklet: *What God Has Joined: A Catholic Teaching on Marriage.* It is published by Basilica Press, Irving, Texas and *Together for Life* by the late Father Joseph M. Champlin. Thousands of couples have used this booklet from Ave Maria Press in their preparation for the reception of their sacrament.

MORE ON MARRIAGE

The lyrics of two songs come to mind. *Love and Marriage* by Sammy Cahn and Jimmy van Heusen. Who can forget Frank Sinatra singing that?!

> "Love and marriage, love and marriage,
> it's an institute you can't disparage.
> Ask the local gentry
> And they will say it's elementary."

The question: Is the local gentry disparaging the institute? It is not elementary anymore. Look at the divorce rate for any couples…Christian or non-Christian!

The other song is from Richard Rogers and Oscar Hammerstein II's musical *Oklahoma*. The song is sung by the characters Will and Annie: *All Er Nothin'*.

Will sings to Annie that before he gives up "wild oats," gambling, and things "a gentleman never mentions…"

> "With me it's all er nuthin'
> Is it all er nuthin' with you?
> It cain't be 'in between'
> It cain't be 'now and then'
> No half and half romance will do!
>
> If you cain't give me all, give me nuthin'
> And nuthin's whut you'll git from me!"

Will expresses the right idea! Marriage demands complete self-surrender of both parties to each other and total fidelity: all or nothing!

In the Book of Revelation there is a verse that covers all the above and much more:

"I wish you were either cold or hot.
So, because you are lukewarm, and neither cold or hot,
I am about to spit you out of my mouth."[59]

---

[59] Revelation 3:15-16

STILL MORE MARRIAGE

The accusation is made: I don't hear priests or ministers talk about marriage from the pulpit. Are they afraid because of the high divorce rate, and, in their audiences, there are so many couples in second civil marriages or so many couples just living together?

Are those the principal reasons?

The Vatican II document on the Church, *Gaudium et Spes, #48* states the following. I think these are powerful and beautiful thoughts on the true meaning of marriage.

> Husband and wife, by the covenant of marriage,
> are no longer two, but one flesh.
> By their intimate union of persons and actions
> they give mutual help and service to each other,
> experience the meaning of their unity,
> and gain an ever deeper understanding of it day by day.
>
> This intimate union in the mutual self-giving of two persons,
> as well as the good of the children,
> demands full fidelity from both,
> and an indissoluble unity between them.
>
> Christ the Lord has abundantly blessed this richly complex love,
> which springs from the divine source of love
> and is founded on the model of his union with the Church.
>
> In earlier times God met his people in a covenant of love and fidelity.
> So now the Savior of mankind, the Bridegroom of the Church,

meets Christian husbands and wives in the sacrament of marriage.

Further, he remains with them in order that,
as he loved the Church and gave himself up for her,
so husband and wife, may, in mutual self-giving
love each other with perpetual fidelity.

Christian partners are therefore strengthened,
and as it were consecrated,
by a special sacrament for the duties and the dignity of their state.
By the power of this sacrament
they fulfill their obligations to each other and to their family
and are filled with the spirit of Christ.
This spirit pervades their whole lives with faith, hope and love.
Thus, they promote their own perfection and each other's sanctification,
and so, contribute together to the greater glory of God.

COMPASSION – NUANCES

Several of the new recording artists have included *Pie Jesus* on their CDs. It is a beautiful song, one I have always admired, from the pen of Lord Andrew Lloyd Webber. He wrote an entire Mass in Latin called *Requiem* in memory of his father, William Lloyd Webber who had passed away in 1982. The Pie Jesus was one of the pieces that many have found beautiful and inspiring. *Pie, Jesus* - Pity, Jesus – Compassion, Jesus.

When we read or hear sacred scripture, we read such phrases as "Jesus was moved with pity." Other traditions will substitute the word "pity" with "compassion" or a similar word. But there are nuances.

- *Pity* – sorrow felt for another person's suffering or misfortune. The etymology of pity is found in the Latin word *pietas*. "Pie" would be the verb, vocative tense: "Pity!"

  The word also has a negative meaning: contempt for someone regarded as inferior or weak.

- *Compassion* – pity accompanied by the desire to help in some way.

- *Commiseration* – deeply felt and openly expressed feelings of pity toward another or group in need.

- *Sympathy* – a Greek word equivalent to compassion. One has similar feelings, understands and is ready to share sorrow.

- *Condolence* – today it is usually a formal expression of sympathy to someone who has experienced death in a family or great sorrow.

The late Redemptorist Priest, Father William McKee has left us a good illustration.

"The compassionate are not in the lifeboat throwing out life preservers to those drowning; they are in the ocean themselves helping the others into the boat or to the safety of the shore."[60]

What about us? Where do we fall on the continuum of compassion? Do the above nuances help us in the identification?

---

[60] Liguori Magazine, March 1983

MORE THOUGHTS ON DIVINE PROVIDENCE

The married Frenchman, Blessed Frederic Ozanam, spoke about divine providence from his early teen years. He told his wife, Amelie, that it was divine providence that brought them together. He was convinced that divine providence was operative throughout his whole life, and it was his responsibility to be open to it – to be alert and prepared to follow it.

Ozanam saw the world as the "workshop of providence." The world created by God was the workshop where God's providence was played out, worked out, and lived out.

Ozanam says that our role is to walk on the path where a merciful providence leads us, to be content to see the stone in front of us whereon to place our foot, without desiring to know the length of the path or the windings of the way.

This married holy man had no doubt: God was operative in every moment of his life. He could reiterate the words of Mother Mary: "Fiat!"

From the writings of Saint Teresa Benedicta of the Cross:

> "Things were in God's plan, which I had not planned at all.
> I am coming to the living faith and conviction that –
> from God's point of view –
> there is no chance and that the whole of my life, down to every detail,
> has been mapped out in God's divine providence
> and makes complete and perfect sense in God's all-seeing eyes."

Do you see the world as the workshop of divine providence?

ZEAL OR DO YOU CALL IT PASSION?

A rose by any other name is a rose. Zeal by any other name is zeal.

I don't hear many preaching about zeal. It is a virtue and very much needed in our spiritual repertoire. We could call it zeal or passion – or could we call it "fire"?

I like what Saint Vincent de Paul says about zeal:

> "Zeal consists in a pure desire to become pleasing to God and helpful to our neighbor, zeal to spread the kingdom of God, zeal to procure the salvation of our neighbor. Is there anything in the world more perfect?
>
> If the love of God is a fire, zeal is its flame. If love is a sun, zeal is its ray.
>
> Zeal is unconditional in the love of God."[61]

"Joe Smith" appears before Saint Peter…

> "Where are your wounds?"
> Joe answers: "I don't have any wounds."
> "Was there no passion in your life, Joe, no cause in which you spent and risked yourself that would invite scars?"

---

[61] CCD, Vol 12, #211, p. 250; 22 August 1659

TEMPTATION

Who doesn't know temptations? They come to us daily in a variety of shapes and forms, big and small, lightweight and heavy-duty. "I'm tempted to buy a new car." "I'm tempted to see that movie because I like that actor." "I am tempted to try heroin for the first time." "I'm tempted to punch him in the mouth."

How many artists have recorded the song *Temptation*? Many, from Bing Crosby on down the line. Some will remember Perry Como's version. If you are a Michigan football fan, you will know Michigan Marching Band version of the song; they have been playing it for years!

> "You are temptation and I am yours
> Here is my heart, take it and say that we'll never part
> I'm just a slave, only a slave
> To temptation, I'm your slave."[62]

Our temptations do indeed come to us in various disguises. No one is immune. There is the ever-present temptation to bring God down to our level rather than reaching to his.

There is the temptation to think of prayer as a bargaining tool, to consider faith as a spiritual insurance policy, to prize religion because it makes us look respectable in eyes of others in our community.

And maybe the worse temptation: to try to make God into our image and likeness. We might voice pious bouquets, but we really trust in ourselves first and foremost.

In the Letter of James, we read:

> "Blessed is anyone who endures temptation. Such a one
> has stood the test and will receive the crown of life that
> the Lord has promised to those who love him.
> No one, when tempted, should say, 'I am being tempted
> by God'; for God cannot be tempted by evil and he

---

[62] Music by Nacio Herb Brown and lyrics by Arthur Freed

himself tempts no one. But one is tempted by one's own desire, being lured and enticed by it; then, when that desire has conceived, it gives birth to sin, and that sin, when it is fully grown, gives birth to death. Do not be deceived, my beloved."[63]

What lures me? What entices me? To what am I a slave?

---

[63] James 1:12-16

CINDERELLA

Not too long ago, I saw again a musical presentation of *Cinderella* on television. I was surprised to see it because I didn't know it was still in circulation. I realized that I had seen all three versions of the musical; this was the third version. Whatever version, I have always enjoyed the music by Rogers and Hammerstein!

The story of Cinderella is an old one, but one that still applies to the good in us.

The girl's name is intriguing: *Cinderella*: "the girl who sits in the cinders" – ashes!

We might consider Cinderella as a symbol of Lent. She had a tough life due to her stepmother and her stepsisters. Cinderella seemingly did everything they wanted without complaining, even though she was treated more as a slave than a loving relative.

Cinderella lived an austere life; she sat in the cinders. She carried her crosses daily.

Cinderella sings about her own little corner, her own little chair "where I can be whatever I want to be."

Before the prince puts that glass slipper on her foot, before her marriage, she knew humility. In a sense, Cinderella shows us the dramatic change: a radical difference; a conversion from cruelty and unkindness to happiness and love.

> "Whoever does not take up the cross and follow me is
> not worthy of me.
> Those who find their life will lose it, and those who lose
> their life for my sake will find it".[64]

The prince sings to Cinderella:

---

[64] Matthew 10:38-39

"Do I love you because you're beautiful,
Or are you beautiful because I love you?"

Good question for any close relationship.
Can I apply it spiritually?

HOW MANY PERSONS ARE IN US?

I met Baroness Catherine de Hueck Doherty at Madonna House in Canada while I was studying spirituality in Toronto. She had to be in her 80's. I had met her husband, Eddy Doherty, when I was a young teen at my parish in Chicago. Eddy was then a journalist.

I had read several books she had written because I found them both inspirational and worthy of close reflection.

Catherine had come a long way in life. She was a Russian Baroness who had much and then little. She was that person who found the secret of combining sanctity and wholeness simultaneously, a rare feat for most of us, but certainly our pursuit in life.

The Baroness said that there were three persons inside of her. She had a name for each:

The Baroness: she is spiritual, and the one who practices forms of asceticism and the prayer. She is the one who founded the Madonna House Apostolate, the writer of spiritual books, and the one who tries to give her life to God's poor.

Then there is *Catherine*. She likes doing little and enjoys the nice, creative comforts: long baths, fine clothes, make-up, good wine and food, and as a married woman, a healthy sex life.

She is not into any kind of asceticism, obviously, nor is she religious. She does not like the Baroness; their relationship is very strained to say the least. (I suspect that this persona had memories of her former years as a Baroness: the good life.)

Lastly, there is *the little girl*. This girl enjoys herself on a hillside of Finland, watching the clouds go by; she is a daydreamer.

Catherine said that when she got older, she felt more like the Baroness, longed more for Catherine, but thought that maybe the little girl daydreaming in a Finnish hillside might be who she really was.

How many different persons are there in us?

Where do we stand at this moment in our process of being whole: in harmony and unified?

LIFE 1, DEATH 0

Remember the old adage? There are only two things we can be certain of: death and taxes. Death is inevitable. None of us escape it.

But, as Saint Paul says,

> "Death has been swallowed up in victory.
> Where, O death, is your victory? Where, O death is your
> sting? The sting of death is sin, and the power of sin is
> the law.
> Thanks be to God, who gives us the victory through our
> Lord Jesus Christ."[65]

Many people fear death and do everything in their power to avoid talking about it and avoiding any illness. What happened during the coronavirus pandemic?

Many people refuse to have an open casket at their wakes. This was the wish of one of my sisters. Many people want cremation. Many, however, donate their bodies to science.

Why the fear? What are the reasons?

As we pray, "Life has changed, not ended."

I have witnessed deaths of priests. I have been there with them. It always has been a spiritual experience for me. I also have seen the wonders of hospice care.

We usually are buried in a cemetery. The word comes from the Greek and means "a sleeping place." The word dormitory has the same meaning: a place to sleep. A good number of Christians talk about the "Dormition of the Blessed Mary." She fell asleep and was taken into heaven to join her Son, Jesus.

I have seen a Daughters of Charity cemetery in Japan where the ashes of the deceased Sisters are buried in beautiful urns. And I have experienced burying the ashes of non-Catholics in the Atlantic Ocean.

---

[65] 1 Corinthians 15:54-57

There are numerous ends of life issues. The Catholic Church has excellent guidelines which cover most of a person's concerns and issues.

Again, from my personal experience, the best way to ensure that a person's wishes and their religious beliefs are respected by family and medical personnel, there are two basic essential documents: A Living Will by itself or an Advance Directive with a Durable Power of Attorney (or Proxy) for Health Care Decisions. I have found the latter an absolute for dying priests and the medical profession.

Ms. Peggy Lee's famous song comes to mind by composers Jerry Leiber and Mike Stoller: *Is That all There Is?* If so, "then let's keep dancing."

But we know differently.

There is more. Life has changed, not ended.

DEATH AND DYING

Doctor Elisabeth Kubler-Ross authored a book some years ago which is still talked about: *On Death and Dying.*

From her research, she describes five distinct stages, a process by which people deal with grief and tragedy, especially when a person is confronted by a terminal illness or catastrophic lost. Some recent medical authorities say that the Kubler-Ross theory of stages of grief is invalid. But other studies were consistent with the five-stage theory.

The five stages:

- Denial. "It is not happening to me."
- Anger. "Why me? It is not fair!"
- Bargaining. "I'll do anything you want, God, but first let me see him born." "I know that I'm dying, but could I have more time?"
- Depression. "I'm so sad, why bother with anything."
- Acceptance. "It's okay." "I'm ready." As Father Bob Coerver said to me: "My bags are packed."

All five stages do not necessarily come in sequential order, nor are all five steps experienced by everyone.

The grief process is highly personal and unique for everyone. Nothing should be rushed or forced upon anyone.

Have you seen these stages in anyone?

Are you personally going through one of them?

KIBEHO, RWANDA

I have had the opportunity to visit several African nations, but never Rwanda. I did have a young seminarian in direction from Rwanda; he and his parents miraculously escaped the genocide.

Before the horrific genocide, the Blessed Virgin Mary appeared in Kibeho, Rwanda on 21 November 1981. Her message was similar to that of Fatima and elsewhere: conversion through a life of prayer and confession, a renewal of life by the Word of God, and works of charity and justice. In the apparitions, Mary identified herself as *Mother of the Word*.

Our Lady emphasized recitation of the rosary and particularly the rosary of the Seven Sorrows to obtain the grace of conversion and renewal. The name of the shrine in Kibeho is *Shrine of Our Lady of Sorrows*.

After a long and thorough investigation, the Holy See officially approved the apparitions in 2001, the only Marian shrine in Africa so approved.

Twelve years before the genocide of over a million people in Rwanda, the Blessed Mother warned the visionaries of "a river of blood, people who were killing each other, abandoned corpses with no one to bury them, a tree all in flames, bodies without their heads."

The prediction came true in the spring of 1944 when almost one million Tutsis were murdered, and many beheaded bodies thrown into the Kagea River.

Our Lady has been clear: her warnings were not just for the continent of Africa, but for the whole world. Mary has said that the world is in revolt against God and on the edge of catastrophe.

Mary has invited us to pray, fast, and do penance.

Every September 15 the church celebrates the Feast of the Seven Sorrows of Mary. Perhaps we need to reflect on these more than once a year. Obviously, Mary has more than seven concerns today.

MIRACLES

In Rogers and Hammerstein's musical *Flower Drum Song*, the leading lady sings:

> "A hundred thousand miracles are happ'ning ev'ry day,
> And those who say they don't agree
> Are those who do not hear or see.
> A hundred thousand miracles,
> A hundred thousand miracles are happ'ning ev'ry day."

You and I see miracles daily. As a priest, I act in the person of Christ, and see before my very eyes bread and wine changed into the Body and Blood of Jesus Christ, and then partake of that miracle by receiving Holy Communion.

I hear confessions, and I hear Jesus forgive sin. If you attend the Eucharist, you see the miracle. If you are the one who confesses your sins, you experience the miracle.

Some people of Rwanda, Africa were chanting:

> "Show us a miracle! Make us believe.

One of the male visionaries of the apparitions of Our Blessed Mother at Kibeho, Rwanda told a group assembled at a parish:

> "Our Lord says to stop asking for miracles, because your
> lives are miracles.
> A true miracle is a child in the womb; a mother's love
> is a miracle;
> a forgiving heart is a miracle.
> Your lives are filled with miracles,
> but you're too distracted by material things to see them.
> Jesus tells you to open your ears to hear his messages
> and open your hearts to receive his love.
> Too many people have lost their way

and walk the easy road that leads away from God.

Jesus says to pray to his Mother,

and the Blessed Virgin Mary will lead you to God Almighty.

The Lord has come to you with messages of love and the promise of eternal happiness, yet you ask for miracles instead.

Stop looking to the sky for miracles.

Open your heart to God; true miracles occur in the heart."[66]

Where are we with miracles? Do we see them? Do we see a hundred thousand miracles happening every day?

---

[66] Segatashya's voice in Our Lady of Kibeho, by Immaculee Ilibagiza, p.xvi, Hays House, Inc.

THE MEDAL OF THE IMMACULATE CONCEPTION

My favorite Marian shrine sits in the midst of the city of Paris. The Shrine of the Miraculous Medal. It is located close to the famous Bon Marche department store on the corner of rue du Bac and rue de Sevres. Hundreds of people come to this sacred ground to attend mass, or go to confession, or pray in silence. It is more than inspiring!

Over the years, during international meetings or pilgrimages, I have had the opportunity of celebrating the Eucharist there or merely to sit in a quiet pew and pray.

On 18 July 1830, the Blessed Virgin Mary first appeared to a new young novice of the Daughters of Charity of St Vincent de Paul. The young novice, Catherine, was known to her family as Zoe Laboure. She would become known to the world as Saint Catherine Labouré.

During this first apparition, the Blessed Mother Mary told Catherine that she would give her a special mission later.

What is astonishing here is the fact this young woman, 24 years old, spent several hours talking to Mary, kneeling at the chair on which Our Lady sat and Catherine rested her hands on Mary's knees. This is incredible but true!

The apparition of 27 November 1830 took place on Saturday evening, the eve of the first Sunday of Advent. Mary gave Catherine her mission. Mary appeared standing on a globe and holding a globe in her hands as if offering it to heaven.

Streaming from rings on Our Lady's fingers were rays of light. Mary explained that these rays symbolized the graces she obtains for those who ask for them. However, some of the rings were dark; these were graces obtainable but did not come forth because no one asked for them.

The apparition switched from Mary standing on the globe to her hands now outstretched and with the dazzling rays of light streaming from her fingers. Framing the figure of Our Lady were the words:

"O Mary conceived without sin, pray for us who have recourse to thee."

It is what we know today as the front of the Miraculous Medal, which is truly the *medal of the Immaculate Conception*. Yet, remember, this was 1830 and the Church did not officially proclaim the dogma until 1854, twenty-four years later!

The vision turned and showed the back of the medal: twelve stars encircling a large "M" from which arose a cross. Below are two hearts with flames coming forth from them. One heart is encircled in thorns and the other pierced by a sword.

It is not difficult to see the biblical significances in these symbols.

Catherine was told by Mary to have the medal struck on this model, and after their approval by the Archbishop of Paris, the first were distributed in 1832. Catherine's confessor, Father Jean-Marie Aladel, C.M., was the one responsible for executing the project. No one knew to whom the Blessed Mother appeared until shortly before Catherine's death on 31 December 1876.

Mary said:

"Come to the foot of this altar and here graces will be bestowed upon all who ask with confidence and fervor. They will be given to the rich and to the poor."

Do we come to the foot of the altar and pray for grace?

Are we wearing the Miraculous Medal around our neck for the right reasons and not just for a nice piece of jewelry or because of superstition?

CONTEXT

I have found out through trial and error that a good thing to do is to put things into context. Things that are pressing, or things that others are frantic about, when put into context, take on a different value or hue. For example, when some seminarian complained about the food, I would ask him if he knew there were over a billion men and women dying of starvation as we spoke. Any one of those billion would love to get their hands on the meal in question.

You can come up with your own examples.

There is a Latin scholastic term which might help: *sub specie aeternitatis* – (under the aspect of eternity).

It is an excellent way of looking at what I'm doing right now – what decisions that I might have to make. From past experience each one of us knows that we made some bad decisions, or fast choices without enough forethought or prudence.

Here are three good questions for "under the aspect of eternity."

They make a good examen of consciousness:

1. Is this going to help me get to heaven or is it going to increase my chances for hell?
2. Is this going to assist my salvation, or is it going to do me harm?
3. How will this appear on the day when Jesus returns in majesty, judge of the living and the dead?

The choices are mine to make based "under the aspect of eternity."

We start the Church's liturgical year with Advent: a beginning. The utilization of putting things in proper context or under the aspect of eternity is a good spiritual practice for the whole year, not just for the four Sundays of Advent.

WHO/WHAT FASCINATES US?

As I had mentioned previously, I had the opportunity of visiting Madonna House at the Combermere, Ontario, Canada while I was studying in Toronto. Baroness Catherine de Hueck Doherty, the foundress, was still alive.

A member of the community, Father Gene Fulton, tells the story of his first day at the Madonna House community. After arriving, he went to chapel to say a prayer, and there prostrated on the floor in prayer was the Baroness Catherine. She was in a mode of adoration and, occasionally, Father Fulton heard her sighs.

Before he knew it, he felt a hand on his shoulder. It was the Baroness. She led him to the tabernacle and said to him:

> "Dear Father, would you place your hands on my head and bless me?"

Then she told the priest:

> "Bow low here and do not ever be fascinated by anyone or anything but Jesus Christ. You will be saved from all illusions in life if you come before his presence."

This is a wonderful principle to live by: don't be fascinated by anyone or anything but Jesus Christ. We can be and are sucked into people and things. Look at how so many follow every detail of a celebrity: television or movie star, rock star, athlete or even certain politicians.

Soren Kierkegaard, a Danish theologian, differentiates between admiration and imitation. We don't admire Jesus, we imitate him. I am afraid that we admire some people too much and then find out that their feet are made of clay; that inside there is much going on that shouldn't be for the sake of the individual.

What fascinates us more than Jesus? Who is it? What is it?

AN EXAMPLE: HOW ONE SAINT PRAYED

One of the disciples of Jesus requested,

> "Lord, teach us to pray, as John taught his disciples."
> (Luke 11:1)

People are still asking: "Teach me to pray!" "How does one pray?"

Saint Catherine Labouré, the Daughter of Charity of Saint Vincent de Paul, has given us a great example.

As I mentioned earlier, she is the saint to whom the Blessed Mother appeared five times in Paris. She is a religious sister who spent forty-six years caring for senior men of Enghien, an area of Paris. No one knew that she was the recipient of the apparitions except her confessor.

Her body was exhumed fifty-seven years after her death and found in perfect condition. Her body is encased in the Chapel of the Miraculous Medal in Paris.

We have great descriptions of prayer from the pens of Saint Teresa of Avila, Saint John of the Cross and many modern spiritual authors. Their writings are quite detailed.

Here is the method of prayer that is simple and humble from the lips of Saint Catherine Labouré. Her simplicity endears her to millions. She is a saint of ordinary people who became a saint not because of the apparitions, but by doing her commonplace duties well for the love of God and for those old, crusty men.

> "Whenever I go to the chapel,
> I put myself in the presence of our good Lord,
> and I say to him 'Lord, I am here.
> Tell me what you would have me do.'
>
> If he gives me some task,
> I am content and I thank him.

If he gives me nothing, I still thank him
since I do not deserve to receive anything more than
that.

And then, I tell God everything that is in my heart.
I tell him about my pains and my joys,
and then I listen.

If you listen, God will also speak to you,
for with the good Lord, you must both speak and listen.

God always speaks to you
when you approach him plainly and simply."

KINGDOM

A priest friend of mine voiced his opinion that the Kingdom of God is the end and the Church is the means. Perhaps this needs some finessing. The Kingdom is larger than the Church. The Church is the servant or, if you prefer, the instrument of the Kingdom.

If we delve into sacred scripture, we see that Jesus' primary goal was not to establish the church, but to promote and manifest the Kingdom of God. He said in the beginning of Saint Mark's Gospel that the kingdom of God has come near.[67]

"My kingdom is not from this world."[68]

In the Preface of the Mass for the Feast of Christ the King, we pray:

> "Father,
> You anointed Jesus Christ, your only Son...
> as the eternal priest and universal king...
> As priest he offered his life on the altar of the cross
> and redeemed the human race...
> As king he claims dominion over all creation,
> that he may present to you, his almighty Father,
> an eternal and universal kingdom:
> a kingdom of truth and life,
> a kingdom of holiness and grace,
> a kingdom of justice, love, and peace."

A kingdom is defined as a restricted area containing a people subject and ruled by a lord or monarch, one who makes the laws of the land and rewards all who faithfully serve him.

The Kingdom of God is somewhat analogous. God as king and lord rules over us, his subjects. We obey his laws and he rewards us for our fidelity with his gracious mercy.

---

[67] Mark 1:15
[68] John 18:36

Remember the covenant centuries ago? "I will be your God and you will be my people."[69]

The Kingdom is universal: it assembles together all God's people throughout the world; God rules us and cares for us out of his infinite, unconditional love.

Saint Vincent de Paul said that the Kingdom of God is within us; we start there, then we begin spreading and expanding that Kingdom.

Has the Kingdom taken root in you?

---

[69] Lev. 26:3-13

LENT IS SCHOOL TIME

I have been living in a secondary academic setting for some years now. What has helped me is to see Lent's similarity to an academic year.

Most colleges start off their new school year with orientation for new students and those transferring from other institutions. Lent starts with an orientation: Ash Wednesday to Saturday inclusive. The orientation covers the main themes of Lent: conversion, mortification, prayer, and acts of charity.

Lent follows a "two semester school year."

During the first semester, the Church covers the basics of the spiritual life.

The second semester has all its gospels from the Gospel of Saint John. We see growing animosity toward Jesus: the authorities want him dead.

Lent ends not with final exams, but the final days of Jesus. We celebrate the Sacred Triduum. Although there are different ways of considering these three days, one is to see the unconditional and total love of God for us —and his gifts.

On Holy Thursday, Jesus gives us the Sacraments of his Body and Blood and the ordained Priesthood. On Good Friday, he gives his earthly life away for our sins and the sins of our family and the sins of our friends. On Holy Saturday, after his wake service, he rises from the dead and gives himself to us in his risen body, his glorified body. He gives us this gift of hope: we too will be resurrected!

As Saint Augustine said:

"We are an Easter people and alleluia is our song."

HOW TO GIVE: THE EXAMPLE OF THE WIDOW

Thank God for the generosity of people! Thank God for those men and women who give from their surplus to assist others! Their acts are acts of charity, and, many times acts of justice.

We have an excellent example of another type of giving:

> "Jesus looked up and saw rich people putting their gifts into the treasury.
> He also saw a poor widow put in two small copper coins.
> He said, 'Truly I tell you, this poor widow has put in more than all of them;
> for all of them have contributed out of their abundance, but she out of her poverty has put in all she had to live on."[70]

We give out of our stockpile, bank accounts, and foundations for good causes, to many charities and causes that we particularly like. That is all well and good. And, again, these are wondrous acts of charity.

The unnamed widow gives from her poverty, from her substance. She threw into the temple treasury all that she had to live on. Irresponsible? Not a very bright move? Probably, but she was honoring God with the equivalent of herself and trusting in divine providence – that God would take care of her, that someone would come into her life and give her food and drink.

We had a clothes drive at our seminary. Boxes were placed at the end of several wings of the complex. I put in a good number of things, including good shoes and unused clothing. But was I giving out of poverty or out of substance? Or did I give out of excess? These were things that I did not need. In my thinking, there are many people who need good shoes and good clothes; I had enough.

How do we give the majority of the time? From substance or poverty?

P.S. Thank you for all you give and do for others!

---

[70] Luke 21:1-4

THE CROSS

I have found out what most people know: don't look for a cross; it will find you. The cross has had no trouble in finding me.

The shadow of the cross permeates our lives, Christians and non-Christians, believers and non-believers. We know the cross. As Saint Paul has told us: "a stumbling block to Jews, and foolishness to Gentiles; but to those who are the called…Christ the power of God and the wisdom of God."[71]

The cross takes the form of sickness, old age, loneliness, depression, discouragement, interior trials, worries about loved ones, or torments of our heart.

The wood of cross can come in different colors: tears from the depth of our being, the anxiety of rejection, the worries of unemployment and no finances to keep the family together. The wood of the cross stings and hurts from its slivers: the inability to help others through charity and justice because of external restrictions.

Jesus Christ looks down at us from the cross. The cross expresses the universality of Christ's redemptive love for us. As he hangs there, he sweeps across the ages, the nations. His arms are outstretched to embrace everyone in a gesture of love and mercy.

As Origen said:

> "Where man is concerned, God suffers a passion born of love."

Can we look upon the cross as joyful in any stretch of the imagination? Yes.

We see the joy of the cross in the radical love of God for all humanity. It is an eternal love, an unconditional love, and a total love. It is a love impossible to remain indifferent or powerless in the face of human need and suffering.

---

[71] 1 Cor. 1:23-24

We see the joy of the cross in the faithful love of Jesus who gave his life as a total immolation to redeem us. We see the joy of the cross in knowledge that good does triumph over evil, justice does win over injustice, peace over warfare, love over hatred, and life over death. We see the joy of the cross as an instrument of being able to give for the good of others.

The cross is mystery. The cross is a sign of contradiction.[72]

Jesus says it:

> "No one has greater love than this, to lay down one's life
> for one's friends."[73]

I see this in married couples; I see it in single men and women. I see it in priests and religious. I see it in persons who run non-profit organizations to meet the needs of others.

How many people carry their cross – crosses in a spirit of God's love?

---

[72] 1 Cor. 1:23
[73] John 15:13

CHARITY AND JUSTICE

The Lord hears the cry of the poor. I have to believe that cry, among other things, is for justice. From my limited experience, I see injustices galore perpetrated by the wealthy and powerful. For too many, corruption is their middle name.

The Catholic French scholar said:

> "The order of society is based on two virtues: charity and justice. However, justice presupposes a lot of love already, for one needs to love a person a great deal in order to respect that one's rights, which limit our rights, and that one's freedom, which hampers our freedom. Justice has its limits, whereas charity knows none."[74]

Blessed Frederic Ozanam and others were highly criticized for their charity. Blessed Mother Teresa of Calcutta was one of those. Critics said that persons like Ozanam and Teresa were wasting their time in helping the poor with food, clothing, etc. They should be spending all their energy on the root causes of injustice. The dilemma: you can't allow people to starve or freeze to death while you or someone else is fighting with government officials over grave injustices. Both are needed: charity and justice.

The fact is that Frederic Ozanam wrote a series of newspaper articles in *The New Era* of Paris in 1848 that contain some of the best Catholic social justice material ever written. At Ozanam's beatification ceremonies, Pope John Paul II said:

> "We see in him a precursor of the social doctrine of the Church which Pope Leo XIII would develop some years later in the Encyclical *Rerum Novarum*."[75]

Charity and justice: they go together. Our job is not to forget that and act accordingly.

---

[74] Christianity and Civilization by Blessed Frederic Ozanam, p.8
[75] Pope John Paul II, 22 August 1997

PRUDENCE

It's weird how we remember certain definitions of some things and not others. The definition of prudence is one that I have remembered over the years: *the right way of doing.* As our philosophy books were in Latin – a two volume textbook by the Benedictine Father Joseph Gredt--the definition literally was: *ratio recta agabilia.*

The modern definitions of prudence are "practical wisdom," "practical judgment," or "rational choice."

Here is an example of a prudent person, a person of practical wisdom:

> A prudent person looks at a specific situation before him/her objectively. Then that person applies moral truths, and these may be one or more of the Ten Commandments or the teachings of the Church. (Notice the practicality involved in these steps.) The person makes a moral judgment…yes or no. The action follows: he/she does it or doesn't do it. It is a given that a prudent person will do whatever he or she does in a good way.

The late Pope Benedict XVI spoke about "prudence as searching for the truth and acting in conformity with it. The prudent person is first and foremost a man or woman of truth and of sincere reason. We judge on the basis of the whole, not parts."[76]

Prudence can be seen as the preventive virtue. The acquisition of prudence is like our doctor who practices preventive medicine; he prevents us from a possible serious illness. It is a virtue that forestalls hurried action, slows down our wagon train, calculates possible consequences of our actions, and yet demands action when it is the right time to act.

Prudence: *ratio recta agabilia.*

God grant us the virtue of prudence!

---

[76] Homily, 12 September 2009

FORTITUDE

Fairy tales usually end with the words, "they all lived happily ever after." But real life stories are not fairy tales, and they are not quite so simple.

Consider the Blessed Virgin Mary. She had her struggles as anyone. The old gentleman Simeon prophesied that a sword would pierce her heart, and it did. When Jesus was twelve years old, she experienced a parent's worst nightmare: her son disappeared for three days! What happened to him? Was he kidnapped and sold into slavery? Was he hurt and lying in some stranger's home? What happened to him? After his public ministry, she stood at the foot of the cross and saw what the Roman authorities had done to his body. She heard him take his last breath.

What kept Mary going? Certainly, the virtue of fortitude.

Sometimes people call the cardinal virtue of fortitude "courage," but I like the phrase that the late Pope Benedict XVI used: *spiritual vitality*.

How we need it to live out our Christian vocation to the fullest!

According to the Catechism of the Catholic Church, fortitude is the moral virtue that ensures firmness in the difficulties of life and constancy in the pursuit of the good. It strengthens our resolve to resist the temptations that bombard us. It strengthens us, also, in overcoming the obstacles in the moral life that pop up so often.

Fortitude enables us to conquer fear, including fear of death which so many have. It enables us to face the trials and persecutions that befall so many all over the world.

> It disposes a person even to sacrifice his or her life for the faith or stand up for what is right and just.[77]

We need spiritual vitality – fortitude – for daily living!

---

[77] Catechism of the Catholic Church, # 1808

TEMPERANCE

Temperance...you can call it moderation if you want; some do.

Temperance is the moral virtue that moderates (tempers) our attraction of the pleasures of the senses and provides balance in our use of created goods.

It ensures our will's mastery over our instincts and keeps desires within the limits of what is honorable.

"The temperate person directs one's sensitive appetites toward what is good and maintains a healthy discretion."[78]

Having laid the background for temperance, we must confess that it is not a popular virtue, although it has a remarkable existence in movements: diets, health foods, and programs to help control alcohol, smoking, sex, and narcotics.

We need to cultivate moderation...temperance. Stop and think about the abuse of the environment, material goods, and food. How much food do we throw out every day? I am happy to see some businesses giving their leftovers to agencies that care for the needy like the Society of Saint Vincent de Paul.

What about taking care of ourselves in body, mind, and spirit?

What about temperance and generosity?

---

[78] Catechism of the Catholic Church, #1809, #1838

LABOR DAY

Most humans work and work hard for their daily bread. I have seen it in several countries of the world. As God says in Genesis:

> "By the sweat of your face
> you shall eat bread until you return to the ground,
> for out of it you were taken:
> you are dust, and to dust you shall return."[79]

Our American Bishops annually release a statement for Labor Day. I have found that these statements contain good material for our reflection.

The first Labor Day was celebrated on 5 September 1882 to commemorate the social and economic achievements of American workers and to give them a day off. Labor Day became identified as the last official day of summer, and it signaled the beginning of a new school year for many children.

Labor Day is a day to acknowledge the dignity of work and workers.

The Book of Genesis presents God as creator, working for six days in the creation of the world and the first human beings. He took the seventh day off.

Saint Joseph, the foster father of Jesus, was a carpenter by trade and supported the Holy Family by his income. Jesus was identified as a carpenter. Several of the apostles were professional fishermen. Saint Paul was a tent maker and proud of the fact that he supported himself by his trade.

In his mission statement at Nazareth, as Jesus launched his public ministry, he expressed his preferential opinion for the working class.

The Church teaches the nobility of work and the necessity of just wages for every worker. We still see a variance with the salaries of men and women.

The late Pope John Paul II taught that all people are called to work together for a just society and just economy which would allow everyone

---

[79] Genesis 3:19

to share in the blessings of God. He also expressed his concern that the greed of a few not make the life of the majority miserable.

Labor Day is a good opportunity for all of us to thank God for the blessing of our lives: spiritual and temporal.

Saint Vincent de Paul reminds us:

> "Let us love God, but let it be with the strength of our arms and the sweat of our brow.

COME, HOLY SPIRIT

When I was in college and theology formation, before we did almost anything, we prayed to the Holy Spirit. The prayer is familiar to many people and still is being recited but perhaps less frequently.

> Come, Holy Spirit, fill the hearts of your faithful,
> and kindle in them the fire of your love.
> Send forth your Spirit, and they shall be created;
> and you shall renew the face of the earth.
>
> O God, you instructed the hearts of the faithful
> by the light of the Holy Spirit.
> Grant us in the same Spirit to be truly wise
> and ever to rejoice in his consolation,
> through Jesus Christ our Lord. Amen.

Our class ordination card was conceived by a Spanish artist. As there were seven of us, the artist drew seven of us with tongues of fire over each of our heads. On our ordination day, we received the Holy Spirit in a special way.

The Holy Spirit is the Paraclete – the one who stands by us – our defense attorney.

The Holy Spirit is our advocate. By the indwelling of the Holy Spirit, we ourselves become advocates of God's presence for others.

The Holy Spirit makes demands on us. You and I must monitor the way we live so that others can see us as advocates.

The late Pope Benedict XVI said in New York:

> "Let us implore from God the grace of a new Pentecost for the Church in America. May the tongues of fire, combining burning love of God and neighbor with zeal for the spread of Christ's kingdom, descend on all present."[80]

---

[80] 19 April 2008, Saint Patrick's cathedral, New York City

SUFFERING REVISITED

There are two particular passages from the late Pope Benedict XVI's Encyclical, *Spe Salvi*, that I like and think are laudable for reflection. The first quote has to do with the reduction of suffering:

> "Certainly, we must do whatever we can to reduce suffering: to avoid as far possible the suffering of the innocent; to soothe pain; to give assistance in overcoming mental suffering." (I think that Pope Benedict is fleshing out – taking to another level – the teachings of Jesus in Matthew 25:31-46.)

The passage continues:

> "These are obligations both in justice and in love, and they are included among the fundamental requirements of the Christian life and every truly human life. Great progress has been made in the battle against physical pain; yet the suffering of the innocent, and mental suffering have, if anything, increased in recent decades."[81]

There is no doubt that we have the obligations, both in justice and in love, as Christians and as human beings to do our part, whatever that is, whatever is our capability, to reduce suffering, especially among the innocent and those suffering from mental aberrations.

But to banish it (suffering) from the world altogether is not in our power. This is simply because we are unable to shake off our finitude, and because none of us is capable of eliminating the power of evil, of sin, which, is a constant source of suffering. Only God is able to do this! Only God, who personally enters history by making himself man and suffering within history.

---

[81] Spe Salvi, #36

You and I can't eliminate suffering from our world any more than you and I can eliminate evil or sin from this world – and to be blatantly honest, from ourselves! How much we would like to reduce and finally eliminate sin in our lives.

The other passage touches on redemptive suffering. The Pope says:

> "The capacity to accept suffering for the sake of goodness, truth, and justice is an essential criterion of humanity, because if my own well-being and safety are ultimately more important than truth and justice, then the power of the stronger prevails, then violence and untruth reign supreme. Truth and justice must stand above my comfort and physical well-being, or else my life itself becomes a lie."[82]

Are we able to accept suffering for such attributes of goodness, truth, and justice? Don't these transcend our personal suffering? Can most people who are suffering so much ever get to that level?

---

[82] Spe Salvi, #38

LESSONS FROM THE CHILEAN MINERS

The world remembers the story of the 33 miners trapped underground for two months. The media did a splendid job of broadcasting and televising the entire event. I read Archbishop Vincent Nicholas of Westminster's homily in a Mass of thanksgiving for the rescue of the men. I would like to share what I read.

There are several lessons this scenario has taught us.

Chileans are people who can work together in the protection of human life.

Thirty-three men struggled to stay together in body, mind, and spirit, in spite of terrible circumstances and without communication with the outside world.

A leader emerged from the men and took charge. He rationed out food and water and initiated routines that enabled the men to survive the ordeal.

A deep sense of solidarity prevailed among the miners; they were in this together.

Above ground, there was a group of men and women who clung to the hope that they could, through their working together, be successful.

When the people at the surface received the note that the men were alive, the nation went into full gear: a corporate effort, without any restrictions.

The President of Chile, Sebastian Pinera, personally took on the cause: success or failure he was in for the long haul.

Chile sought the best technical advice from around the world and these experts responded.

The families of the miners were with them in prayer and in spirit. Again, solidarity. As one of the miners said:

> "There were not 33 of us in the mine. There were 34, for the Lord was with us."

As the miners reached the surface, some fell to their knees in thanksgiving to God for their rescue.

Chile showed the world its soul: noble, courageous, steadfast, and faith filled.

What can we take from these lessons for personal or communal application?

WHO DO YOU SAY THAT I AM?

Catholic spirituality starts with Jesus. Jesus is the starter or, as documents say, the author. He is the alpha. And Jesus is the end, the perfecter, the finisher, and the omega.

Pope John Paul II called Jesus "the center of gravity."

Saint Vincent de Paul told his disciples: "Jesus is the center of our life and ministry."

Saint Augustine writes in the person of Jesus:

> You seek me for worldly motives, not for spiritual ones.
>
> How many people seek Jesus solely for worldly ends?
> Rarely does someone seek Jesus for the sake of Jesus.

I was thinking this may well be one of the distinguishing characteristics of holy people juxtaposed others: they seek Jesus just for Jesus, and not because they want something from him.

Jesus asks the question several times during the liturgical year: "Who do you say that I am?"

And your answer is? _____.

Is Jesus your alpha and omega?

Is Jesus your center of gravity?

A SENTENCE THAT MAKES ME PAUSE

Blessed Mother Teresa once said:

> "He (God) will use you to accomplish great things on the condition that you believe much more in his love than in your weaknesses."[83]

That is a WOW statement. I really would like to think that I believe more in God's love than in my weaknesses. But do I? Yes, I believe in his love, but do I spend too much time on my weaknesses? Of course, when I do this, I am spending a lot of time and energy on me, rather than on God.

I don't think about the first part of the sentence: "God will use me to accomplish great things..." Blessed Teresa throws in a conditional clause: "On condition that..."

Do I think of myself accomplishing great things? No. Do I think of myself accomplishing things? Oh, yes. What does Mother Teresa mean by "great things"?

I really need to put more time and effort in believing in God's love than in me and my weaknesses.

If I am honest, I get tired concentrating on weaknesses.

What about you?

---

[83] Life in The Spirit, 1983

HOPE # 2

I was rector of the theologate when it happened...as a consequence of a horrific accident on an icy highway outside of Youngstown, Ohio, Michael Esswein became a quadriplegic. After weeks of surgeries and re-hab, his parish of St. Stephen's in Saint Louis had a night of thanksgiving. Michael wheeled up the aisle; you could hear a pin drop.

Thanksgiving for what? This young man is a quadriplegic.... his promising future is done. This is hardly an answer to our prayers!

Michael preached with example and words:

> "Like the apostles in the gospel in the midst of the storm,
> we are tempted to think our Lord is asleep....
>
> Hope, my friends; hope is the gift that keeps us going
> when we think Jesus is asleep and let us thank God for
> that great gift of hope!"

Michael Esswein went on to be ordained a priest for the Archdiocese of St. Louis. He is now a pastor in the St. Louis area. He never gave up hope!

WORLD AIDS DAY

Having lived in East Africa for a time, I am quite aware of HIV-AIDS. I saw the pandemic in reality, not in journalism. I saw the fabulous ministry done with DREAM in collaborative effort between the two international groups: The Community of Sant'Egidio and the Daughters of Charity of Saint Vincent de Paul in Kenya and Cameroon.

The DREAM Project was conceptualized by the Community of Sant'Egidio. DREAM stands for DRUG RESOURCE ENHANCEMENT against AIDS and MALNUTRITION. The program is designed to help prevent the transmission of HIV/AIDS from an infected mother to her newborn child. The program is holistic, with components of education, HIV/AIDS prevention, drug treatment, ongoing care, balanced nutrition, and personal counseling. The program is free of cost.

The Sant'Egidio Community collaborates also with the Daughters of Charity in Mozambique, Nigeria, and the Congo besides Kenya and Cameroon. Sant'Egidio collaborates with other religious communities in five other African countries.

Each year World AIDS Day is celebrated, an initiative of the United Nations, to call attention to the scourge of AIDS and to invite the international community to renew its commitment in the work of prevention and assistance to those men and women affected.

The Catholic Church has always considered care of the sick as an integral component of her mission in the world. The Church does all it can to fight AIDS through its institutions and dedicated health care professionals.

As members of the Mystical Body of Christ, each is asked to do whatever they can through prayers and actual care for those suffering from the HIV virus and for their families.

THE EUCHARIST

The Eucharist is the source, center, and summit of the Christian life, because in the Blessed Sacrament is contained the whole spiritual food of the church – Christ himself. By the Eucharistic celebration we already unite ourselves with the heavenly liturgy and anticipate eternal life. In brief, the Eucharist is the sum and summary of our faith.[84]

Catholics believe that Jesus Christ is present in the Eucharist: Body, Blood, soul, and divinity under the appearances of bread and wine. It is not a symbol; it really is Jesus Christ!

Two examples of priests under prison terms perhaps testify to the *Real Presence* better than any doctrinal or dogmatic explanation.

Archbishop Francis Xavier Nguyen van Thuan of Vietnam was imprisoned by the Communists in his country for 13 years, 9 years in solitary confinement. While in prison, with the help of several prison guards, he made a small cross out of wood which he hid in his soap. He was able to secure some wine under the pretense of medicine. The archbishop would say Mass from memory using his hand as the chalice using three drops of wine and one drop of water.

The Jesuit, Father Walter Ciszek, was imprisoned for 23 years in the Russian slave labor camps in Siberia. He celebrated Mass with wine made out of raisins (grapes) that they were able to steal. He used the back of a gold watch for the paten, and a small shot glass for the chalice.

These two holy priests knew the power of the Eucharist. They understood it as the source, center, and summit of the spiritual life. They knew how they needed the Body and Blood of Jesus Christ to keep them spiritually alive as they experienced, like Jesus himself, man's inhumanity to man.

---

[84] Catechism of the Catholic Church, #1324-27

PRAYER

Blessed Mother Teresa of Calcutta was criticized, for insistence, that her Sisters pray for two hours a day in chapel instead of using some of that time for ministry to the dying on the streets.

Her answer:

> "If the Sisters did not pray two hours a day, they probably would never go into the streets at all."

Saint Vincent de Paul said:

> "Give me a man of prayer and he will be capable of everything. He may say with the apostle, 'I can do all things in him who strengthens me.'"[85]

At the vigil of Saint Vincent de Paul's 250th anniversary of his canonization, I heard Saint Pope John Paul II say of Saint Vincent:

> "It was not love for men that led him to sanctity; rather,
> it was sanctity that made him truly and effectively charitable;
> It was not the poor that gave him to God but, on the contrary,
> God who gave him to the poor.

Any follower of Jesus Christ has to be a woman or man of prayer. Prayer nourishes action; action nourishes prayer. It is mutuality…one influences and impacts the other. One strengthens the other. Grace builds on nature.

---

[85] CCD, Vol. 11, #67, p. 76

One final quote from Saint Vincent de Paul:

> "If we remain in charity, if we succeed in our work, it is thanks to meditation; if we do not fall into sin, it is thanks to meditation; if we are saved, all this is thanks to God and meditation."[86] (CCD, Vol. XI, 407)

---

[86] CCD, Vol. XI, 407

COLORS OF MARTYRDOM

Martyrdom comes in different colors.

We know red martyrdom – those women and men who shed their blood for the faith.

White martyrdom is those men and women who live their lives day in and day out despite the difficulties, hardships, and crosses of life, including persecution and severe restrictions on the practice of their faith. I understand the Irish call this type *green martyrdom*.

Bearing witness (the word "martyr" in Greek means "witness") to Christ by loving those who hate us, by showing mercy and compassion to those who hurt and ill-treat us is white or green martyrdom. By forgiving those who constantly offend us, by accepting our suffering without complaint, is white or green martyrdom.

Saint Vincent de Paul tells the Daughters of Charity:

> "To consecrate one's life to God in service to the most abandoned people on earth, isn't that going into martyrdom? Yes, without any doubt. Undoubtedly...
> to have one's head chopped off is a bad experience which is over pretty soon.
> And even if they should endure greater torments, these would still not last very long. They would instantly be terminated by death.
> But such young ladies as give themselves to God in your community
> do so to be now among sick people full of infection and wounds
> and often very bad-tempered,
> then with poor children for whom they must do everything....
> O my Daughters, let us hold them in high esteem,
> let us maintain that esteem for them whatever may happen,

let us look upon them as martyrs of Jesus Christ,
because they are serving the neighbor out of love for
him. [87]

What about the single life?
What about married life?
Are these not examples of white martyrdom?

---

[87] Conferences #15 and #27

WHERE HAVE ALL THE MANNERS GONE?

I read an article in USA Today: "Manners Still Matter." My immediate reaction was: Yes!

I remember that we occasionally had an etiquette class in seminary formation, which many of us found boring but, as I look back, I am delighted we had.

Every year, close to the beginning of the academic year, the seminary administration where I ministered brought in an etiquette expert to take the entire community through a fully dressed table and meal. The expert walks everyone through the meal course by course, interspersed with questions, either initiated by him/her or by the students. I dare say that one significant reason for this session is because the students are not getting much at home in the way of proper table etiquette.

Where have all the manners gone? Manners still matter. Is anyone teaching good manners or do we need to have workshops or seminars and pay good money?

I find many young people on streets, in stores, or in malls to be rude or totally oblivious to others. It is as if you were invading their air space. I rarely hear: "Excuse me," "Pardon me," "I'm sorry," and "Thank you." Where have these gone?

Is there a connection between proper etiquette, good manners, and charity?

Doesn't etiquette and manners respect the dignity of the person?

HERE COMES THE JUDGE

A priest acquaintance told me this story recently. A world-renown actor came to the rectory with regards to an upcoming baptism. The people in the parish office did not recognize him and thought that he was a homeless man seeking assistance because he was so poorly dressed and shabby looking. It took some "acting" on the man's part to get the staff to realize why he was there.

How do you judge people? By how they dress and groom themselves?

By how much you think that they have in the bank?

By how many cars, homes, possessions they have or vacations they take?

Jesus has given the criteria for judgment; it is spelled out in Matthew 25:31-46.

We need to keep reminding ourselves how difficult it is to give ourselves in love and genuine concern, because these things are far costlier than writing out a check or slipping someone cash from our wallet or purse.

And then there are:

- our inner motives and intentions (the internals are always difficult to judge!)
- the degree of our surrender to God's will.
- the sacrifices we make for others (the externals are easier to judge, but we need to take it slow).

BAD OFF?

Bob had recently moved to New York City for business purposes. On his first day there, he took the subway to meet a client. After the subway car was closed and the train started, he heard a saxophone and here comes a visually challenged gentleman moving toward his end of the subway car. Attached to the bottom of the sax was a small plastic cup for donations.

As the man made his way through the car, Bob noticed that it was the poorer types putting coins into the cup, not the men in three-piece suits carrying briefcases. It was the poor helping the poor. It was as if they were saying:

> "We might be poor, but not so bad off that it prevents us from helping someone in need."

Remember the story of the poor widow in the Temple? She put into the treasury the only two coins she had.

Are we ever that bad off that we just can't help someone else in any way whatsoever?

BLOOD IS THICKER THAN FAITH?

We saw it in Rwanda: the genocide, tribe against tribe, when a million people were massacred. Hutu killing Tutsi; Catholics killing Catholics. I saw it in Kenya: the same thing. Members of the Catholic Church killed other Catholics because of tribal differences: Luos, Kalenjin and others vs Kikuyu—and vice versa.

One of the Rwandan bishops said it best:

> "This proved unfortunately that for our Christians, blood was much thicker than the water of baptism."

I heard Kenyans telling stories months later after the chaos and turmoil of seeing men attending Sunday Mass, the same men who butchered or raped or destroyed homes of their fellow Catholic families. Blood is thicker than faith.

Can faith ever be thicker than blood?

How thick is your faith?

SIGNS OF THE TIMES

Vatican II issued magnificent documents. One of these was the *Pastoral Constitution on the Church in the Modern World*.[88] It is known for its Latin name: *Gaudium et Spes* – (Joy and Hope).

The first paragraph of the "Introduction: The Condition of Humanity in the World Today" speaks of our responsibility:

> "In every age, the church carries the responsibility of reading the signs of the times and of interpreting them in the light of the Gospel, if it is to carry out its task. In language intelligible to every generation, it should be able to answer the ever recurring questions which people ask about the meaning of this present life and of the life to come, and how one is related to the other."[89]

Pope Benedict XVI voiced his opinion in the opening of the conclave in 2005 that the world is building a dictatorship of relativism that does not recognize anything as definitive and whose ultimate standard consists solely of one's own ego and desires.

This is a sign of the times. What have we done to truth? What have we done to objective truth? The results of this relativism are a new paganism, a new intolerance, the crusade of the atheists, and the clash of two spiritual worlds: the world of faith and the world of secularism.

Do you read the signs of the times or do you presume that the church's hierarchy is doing that – or should do that?

But what about yourselves?

Are you "sign-readers"?

---

[88] Gaudium et Spes; 7 December 1965
[89] Introduction: The Condition of Humanity in the World Today, #4

JOHN THE BAPTIZER

How would you like to be remembered all these centuries by a nickname? That's the case with John, son of Zechariah and Elizabeth. John's father was a priest, who belonged to the priestly order of Abijah.[90] Therefore, John was a priest also because of his dad.

John was eccentric and ascetical. Look at the way he lived! He wore clothes made out of camel's hair and ate locusts and wild honey. And his dwelling was the wilderness: torrid days and breezing nights, open to deadly snakes and wild animals.

His pitch was the same:

"Repent, for the kingdom of heaven has come near.
Prepare the way of the Lord."[91]

You notice that John's target was the individual person. He knew that if individuals changed their lives, then society would be changed and be more human.

People nicknamed John the "Baptizer" because he was putting them through a water ritual to symbolize externally what they were striving for internally: change of heart and action. The word *baptize* in Greek means "to submerge." We could call John the "Submerger."

In my thinking, John is a great example of five virtues:

- *Simplicity*: Again, look at his lifestyle, food, and clothing.
- *Humility*: John never had an identity crisis: he knew who he was and what his mission was.
- *Meekness*: Although he may seem rough and gruff, he had to have certain gentleness about him to attract hundreds of people. People sensed his charity and compassion.

---

[90] Luke 1:15
[91] Matthew 3:1-4

- *Mortification:* This relates to his simplicity, but also his dying to self in order to live for being the precursor of the Messiah.
- *Zeal:* His passion, his zeal, the internal fire within him fueled his life.

John the Baptizer, the priest and son of a priest, was a true missionary. How well do we know ourselves? Where are we?

SOLIDARITY

Earlier, I quoted from the "Introduction to the Pastoral Constitution on the Church in the Modern World" (*Gaudium et Spes* in Latin; *Joy and Hope* in English). The main text starts with these words of solidarity:

> "The joys and hopes, the grief and anguish of the people of our time, especially of those who are poor or afflicted, are the joys and hopes, the grief and anguish of the followers of Christ as well. Nothing that is genuinely human fails to find an echo in their hearts. For theirs is a community of people united in Christ and guided by the Holy Spirit in their pilgrimage toward the Father's kingdom, bearers of a message of salvation for all of humanity. That is why they cherish a feeling of deep solidarity with the human race and its history."[92]

How many of us remember the Polish non-governmental trade union founded by Lech Walesa at the Lenin Shipyards (now *Gdansk Shipyards*) in August 1980? The movement was called "Solidarity." It gave birth to a broad anti-communist nonviolent social movement which, at its peak, brought together 10 million members and vastly contributed to the demise of communism.

The Catholic Church talks about solidarity as one of the seven themes of Catholic social teaching. It sees solidarity as a virtue.

Saint Pope John Paul writes:

> "Solidarity is not a feeling of vague compassion or shallow distress at the misfortunes of so many people, both near and far. On the contrary, it is a firm and persevering determination to commit oneself to the common good, that is to say, to the good of all and each individual, because we are all really responsible for all."[93]

---

[92] Gaudium et Spes; p.1
[93] Pope John Paul: On Social Concern, #38

The relevant question for these signs of the times: "Am I my brother's keeper?" We know these words from the Book of Genesis…they trouble many!

To what extent am I morally and socially responsible for others, especially those who are poor or in need?

What do I understand from the quote above from Saint Pope John Paul II?

A GIFT YOU CAN LOSE

A short time after my first assignment as a priest, I was told about a man who had left the priesthood and became a lawyer. He lived in a small nearby Texas town. When asked why he had not joined some other religious group in his area, his reply was: "I lost my faith, not my mind." I heard, a few years later, that the former priest returned to his faith before he died.

I once played the part of Father Callifer in an amateur production of Graham Greene's play The *Potting Shed.* After all these years, I find myself thinking of that play and re-thinking that part.

Father Callifer in some ways reminds me of the whisky priest in Greene's classic novel *The Power and the Glory* except Callifer, although he likes his whisky too much, seems to be a man who goes through the motions and actions of priesthood, but has lost his faith completely. The dialogue between the priest's housekeeper and himself surely gives you that idea.

But at the end of the scene, we find out from the conversation with his nephew James what transpired. We learn that Father Callifer had been an exemplary priest. As a youth James hung himself, but was resurrected through the prayers of his uncle, the priest. The priest doesn't want to believe it was a miracle because if it were a miracle, God would exist. If God existed, why should God have taken away his faith? For thirty years, he lived out his priesthood in this frame of mind and heart.

It is revealed: Father Callifer had promised God something, something that he valued the most of all, if the boy would live. The priest couldn't remember what he had offered God, but James found it…the thing Father Callifer loved the most. "Take away my faith, but let him live."

It hits Father Callifer like a thunderbolt. He had offered God the one thing that he had loved the most in life: his faith. And God traded him James' life for his faith. As nephew James is helping his "little drunk" uncle to bed, the scene ends with these words from the lips of the priest: "I thought I had lost him forever."

Faith is indeed a gift, a gift from God. We can't take it for granted. We can lose it.

IT TAKES ALL KINDS

A well-published priest psychologist and I were walking down a street in Chicago one afternoon. I don't know how we got on the topic, but he said to me:

> "Ron, wouldn't the world be a better place if there were more people like us? We don't cheat or steal or rob banks or cause violence."

> My immediate response:
> "Yes, but it would be a boring world!"

I can't imagine and would not want to see everyone with a personality and temperament like mine – or like that psychologist's, although I always thought that he had his act together better than I did. While I am outgoing to a certain degree, I have been classified more introvert than extrovert on the Myers-Briggs (I have taken the type indictor four times with the same results).

We need a mixture of introverts and extroverts and everyone in between. We need diverse personalities and temperaments. We need people with vivid imaginations and great creativity. We need dreamers; we need critical thinkers. We need justice-seekers, peacemakers, mourners. We need proclaimers of truth.

We need men and women of character, of compassion, challengers. We need saints. We need men and women of faith!

Who are you in this global village, this global community?

Do you enjoy diversity?

GUILT

I have heard members of various religious denominations boast of their guilt as if it were something to be proud of – as if it were a virtue! Protestants, Jews, and Catholics vie for the number one position in the guilt parade.

I sometimes have thought that Saint Paul should have written:

"Faith, hope, and guilt, and the greatest of these is guilt."
God forbid!

When talking about guilt, we need to make a distinction between "feeling guilty" and "being guilty."

When I do something wrong, I will either stop right there and do nothing or I will do something and move on in my life (e.g., go to confession).

I can simply feel guilty and remain with those feelings – wallow in them like a hog in a poke. If I do, then I am putting stoppage on something positive and good happening in my life.

There is such a thing as justifiable guilt; our immoral behavior warrants such feelings of guilt. For example, I commit adultery, and I feel guilty. Well, I should because I am guilty. To have no sense of guilt after adultery or any serious offense throws up roadblocks in my ability to grow as a human being.

The ability to feel justifiable guilt is an important part of human normality. Sorrow for serious wrongdoing is a vital element of anyone's conscience. And a well-informed active conscience is an important aspect of purity of heart.

A positive response to my justifiable guilt is repentance. I do something in reparation for my sinful (and maybe criminal) action because I am guilty.

Jesus says in the beginning of his public ministry:

"The time is fulfilled, and the kingdom of God has come near.
Repent, and believe in the good news."[94]

---

[94] Mark 1:15

SCRIPTURE ACCORDING TO MARK TWAIN

We certainly don't recognize Mark Twain as a reputable scripture scholar, but he has left us an intriguing quote:

> "Most people are bothered by those passages in scripture which they can't understand; but as for me, I always noticed that the passages in scripture which trouble me most are those that I do understand."

Do you agree?

Which passages do you understand that trouble you most?

Are they the ones about discipleship where Jesus lays down the requirements for being his follower?

Does Jesus expect too much of us in this century?

May the peace of Christ disturb you!

ME

The card came in the mail from an old friend.

One side of the card read:

> Dear Jesus,
> I have a problem.
> It's me.

On the flip side of the card:

> Dear Child,
> I have the answer.
> It's me.

Too simplistic? Or too realistic?
Often the problem is me. As one of my married friends, Ed, told me:

> "Ron, I am a good person, but I do dumb things."

It's the dumb things that cause us problems – and cause us to be a problem.

But Jesus is the answer to our problem and problems.

Do we believe it or are we too often on a quest for some guru or celebrity host?

We look for some new popular book that we heard was just what we probably needed. We hoped that it will show us, step by step, how to live well and be consistently happy.

We watch special presentations on public television searching for answers to life, liberty, and the pursuit of happiness.

What about the four gospels? Therein lies Jesus, the answer.

Are we overlooking the answer right in front of us? The one we already know?

THE WHISKY PRIEST

He's a puzzlement.

For years, I find myself going back to certain paragraphs in Graham Greene's classic *The Power and the Glory*.

The alcoholic priest who fathered a child in some ways mystifies me. He insisted on performing his priestly responsibilities to the end which he knew would come at any time if he was caught by the Mexican authorities.

This fallen priest has much to teach all priests – his imperfection challenges our imperfection – and his adamant adherence to certain spiritual principles say much. I would not be the first one to cast a stone.

A teenage girl asked the whisky priest why he continued to function as a priest, while the Mexican police were breathing down his neck. The conversation went as follows:

> The girl said: "Of course, you could – renounce."
> He said: "I don't understand."
> The girl: "Renounce your faith."
> The priest: "It's impossible. There's no way. I'm a priest. It's out of my power."
> The girl said: "Like a birthmark."

"The vocation and mission received on the day of his ordination mark permanently."[95]

The whisky priest prayed that he be caught soon. And he was. In prison, he expresses his deep remorse: he has been a fool, useless, non-productive of any good.

> "He felt only an immense disappointment because he had to go to God empty-handed...It seemed to him... that it would have been quite easy to have been a saint. It

---

[95] CCC # 1583

- 178 -

would only have needed a little self-restraint and a little courage. He knew now that at the end there was only one thing that counted – to be a saint."[96]

Have you ever felt that: it's easy to be a saint?
In the end, is it the only thing that counts: to be a saint?

[96] Penquin Books, in association with William Heinemann Ltd.; Part 3, chapter 4, p.210

CORE VALUES

Too many of us are *surface-riders* not *core-miners*. They skate on the surface of life. They hug the surface and don't get to the heart of the matter, the core of things.

Some remain with the emotions and ignore the issue underneath. They work the top layers of life and stay there, but refuse to drill further down. I suspect that it is less scary and easier to ride the surface.

Core values are our genetic code – our standards – fundamental principles. They express our heart. The Latin root for *core* is "cor" which means "heart." Core values are the traits or qualities that speak of the driving forces, the priorities of our life.

In organizations, these core values are specified by their vision and mission statements. And many have value statements as well.

What are the core values of your life?

Are you a surface-rider or a core-miner?

Jesus expressed his mission statement at the beginning of his public ministry in the synagogue of Nazareth, as is written in the Gospel of Luke:

> He came to Nazareth, where he had grown up, and went according to his custom into the synagogue on the Sabbath day. He stood up to read and was handed a scroll of the prophet Isaiah. He unrolled the scroll and found the passage where it was written: "The Spirit of the Lord is upon me, because he has anointed me. He has sent me to proclaim liberty to captives and recovery of sight to the blind, and to proclaim a year acceptable to the Lord."[97]

---

[97] Luke 4:16-19

IS GOD TOO ACCESSIBLE?

In Graham Greene's classic *The Heart of the Matter,* Scobie, one of the main characters, reflects after going to confession:

"Is God too accessible?"

Scobie states something that many have found:

There is no difficulty in approaching him (God).

God is open to any of his followers at any hour, 24/7. Look at the corpus on the crucifix, he even suffers in public.

Do you personally find God accessible at any time, day or night? Or do you find God absent most of the time – not available?

What about presumption? If God is so accessible, where does presumption fit in?

For example, I commit a sin of fornication, and I know that I can go to confession tomorrow morning and be forgiven. I presume that I will receive absolution.

God is so accessible because the priest is so accessible for me.

The sins of presumption are against the First Commandment.

The Catholic Catechism speaks about two kinds of presumption: we presume upon our own capacities, hoping to be able to save ourselves without help from God, or we presume upon God's omnipotence or his mercy, hoping to obtain our forgiveness without conversion and glory without merit.[98]

We skate the surface of life. We hug the surface and don't get to the heart of the matter, the core of things. Many live on the parameter of life…we skate the surface!

---

[98] CCC #2092

VACANCY FOR GOD

We see the signs lighted up or placards in windows: "No Vacancy" – "Vacancy."

What about vacancy for God?

An excellent description of celibacy comes from the pen of Saint Thomas Aquinas. He refers to celibacy as *vacare Deo* – to be vacant for God. Or, perhaps, a better translation in English would be: "to be empty for God."

That is a good take on celibacy: to be empty for God so that God may fill us up – so that we may be prepared and ready for God. We are open for service of God's people.

We have to be careful here. Vacancy for God is not limited or restricted to an elite group of men and women. It is an essential part of all Christian lifestyles: priesthood, religious life, marriage, single life, friendship, and communal life.

Celibates do not attach us to any one particular person, and so remind us that relationship with God is the alpha and omega of all human relationships (also the source). Celibates belong to God.

Celibates live out the vacancy in their lives for God by not marrying, by living chaste celibacy, by not accumulating a large bank account, by not filling the vacancy by compensating celibacy with toys and gadgets and people. Celibates strive to be walking, living signs of another kind of intimate love.

How empty are you for God in your vocation?

BURN THE DEVIL!

The people of Guatemala launch the Christmas season with an annual event: *Quema del Diablo* – "Burning of the Devil." Our Vincentian priests and brothers of Guatemala knew the fiesta well. My Guatemalan friends tell me that it is a mixture of Mayan and Catholic religious practices.

The celebration marks the victory of good over evil, unites the people on a national basis, and prepares them for the coming Christmas season.

The *Quema* ritual is celebrated at dusk on December 7th. People clean out their houses, collect their trash, and burn it. The symbolism is evident: purification and freedom from the powers of evil. It is, in many ways, reminiscent of the time when Advent was considered more of a penitential season – a second Lent – than it is now. But *Quema* also looks forward to a new year. What is past is past, get rid of the old, and look toward to the new.

Just before 6:00 pm, the Devil's number (remember 666 from the Book of Revelation?), there is a countdown, like people do in Times Square on New Year's Eve before midnight. At exactly 6:00 pm, someone sets the effigy of the Devil into flames. It has been soaked previously with gasoline. The people shout and cheer and music erupts.

The Devil is burned! *Quema del Diablo!*

But 6:00 pm also indicates First Vespers for the Feast of the Immaculate Conception, a feast of special devotion to the Blessed Virgin Mary and dear to the Guatemalans. The Devil is trampled by the Immaculate Conception!

The morale is: The Devil may cause plenty of trouble during the year, but December belongs to *Los Santos* – "the saints."

ACEDIA: THE NOONDAY DEVIL

Acedia is not a word in our common vocabulary, but the reality is that it is common to our lives, whether people are aware of it or not.

It is a reality well-known among the monks of the early ages. In Greek, *acedia* means "lack of care." The monks knew it as spiritual apathy and torpor rooted in the capital sin of sloth.

I remember it being mentioned in patrology classes. Msgr. Ronald Knox often talked about it in priest retreats. And I am certain that he picked it up from John Cassian or perhaps Evagrius Ponticus from the fourth century. I have talked about it in spirituality classes and in individual spiritual direction.

Two presentations have been Kathleen Norris' *Acedia and Me* and Abbot Christopher Jamison's book, *Finding Happiness*, from the BBC television series *The Monastery*. I highly recommend both resources.

One of the dangerous enemies in our spiritual life is acedia or the noonday devil mentioned in Psalm 91:6.

I think that a good way to describe acedia or noonday devil is spiritual boredom. The deadly sin of sloth induces spiritual slumber. What happens is sadness about the good before us, boredom with the things of God, a failure to respond properly with repentance, zeal, or love to God's goodness. You can understand why men like Cassian and Ponticus tackled the subject and spoke about it often to their monks.

The battle against spiritual sloth is perseverance in prayer, but not just the recitation of prayers, but the practice of mental prayer. This is one of the best solutions promoted from the 4th century. We need to reflect on the truths of our faith, the attributes of God, and the mysteries of Jesus' life to mention but three areas. The noonday devil is close at hand.

Does the spiritual life bore you?

Are you spiritually tired from praying and fighting temptation?

Are you spiritually tired of helping people?

VISIONS AND DREAMS

The famous Bob Dylan was asked by an interviewer about his future plans. Mr. Dylan startled the interviewer:

"I'm looking forward to some dreams.
Excuse me?
It says right there in the Bible.
Dylan explained:
Your young men and women will see visions,
and your older men and women will dream dreams."

"Your young men shall see visions, and your old men shall dream dreams".[99]

I heard that quote from the prophet Joel and from Acts several times during seminary formation. We were young men then, and I suppose our formators expected their words to stir up the imagination and creativity of our youth.

I dare say that we had visions; we saw ourselves as gifted and popular priests doing great things for God. Bishop Fulton Sheen was one of our heroes. While I might never be as bright as he, would that I be as charismatic and appealing to everyone, Christian and non-Christian as he!

Our missionaries in China, then Taiwan, came and spoke to us while on their vacations. Their stories fueled our visions with limitless possibilities.

But youth has evaporated. I am now an "old man" dreaming dreams. What do I dream about? For one, yesteryear memories when I was in better health and thinner! I dream about what I failed to do, what I regret that I have done, of what I wish I could do. But yesterday is past tense, water under the bridge, the future does not exist; all I have is now, the present tense.

I dream of those men and women who touched my life in a myriad of ways – good, bad, and ugly, but especially for the good. How blessed I

---

[99] Acts 2:17; Joel 2:28

have been to have met them and interacted with so many people in this world.

I dream of my deceased siblings, Bill, Bev, Jeanne, and Lucille who have gone before me marked with the sign of faith. I can never forget my mother, Lucille, and stepdad, Bill, who raised me. How I wish they were physically alive and available for sharing my stories. I am no longer young, but young at heart.

Does God have visions for you?

Does God have dreams for you?

EVANGELIZATION

A "Speakers' Corner" is an area open to public speaking, discussion, and debate. Hyde Park, London, claims the original Corner, although now four other London parks have areas designated as Speakers' Corners. Here people speak on any subject, as long as the police judge the material lawful.

A person says whatever he or she wants – matters important to the speaker and what he or she wants to make known to the public, to whoever will listen.

For us Christians, the whole world is our Speakers' Corner. Our mandate from Jesus is to announce his good news. We can preach it with words or better still, through the example of our lives.

Our mandate comes from our reception of Baptism and Confirmation: to continue his mission, to spread his good news. We are to be evangelizers. The word *evangelium* means "good news." An evangelizer is an announcer of good news.

We know how much bad news is on the daily news programs. It is refreshing to hear good news.

Evangelization is a two-way street. Evangelizers evangelize, but it is active and passive. It is give and take. Those we evangelize, evangelize us in the process.

Are we open? Are we receptive?

A SAINT: ANOTHER LOOK

I was fortunate to have been a participant in the First Worldwide Priest Retreat in Rome. There were 6,000 of us from every country and island of this hemisphere.

I am still quite amazed at the list of speakers we had:

Saint Pope John Paul II
Saint Teresa of Calcutta
Leon Joseph Cardinal Suenens
Raniero Cardinal Cantalamessa, O.F.M. Cap.
Bernardin Cardinal Gantin
and others less well-known.

Cardinal Suenens, at the time, was in his 80's, but still active. He had been a major player at Vatican II, one of its principal architects. The church owes him much.

The Cardinal talked to us about "Holiness: Normal Christianity in the Power of the Holy Spirit." The Cardinal began his presentation with a story:

On a previous special occasion, a journalist asked him:
"What is a saint?"
Suenens' immediate reply without thinking:
"A saint is a normal Christian, no more, no less. The only trouble is that the rest of us are far too abnormal."

Do you think that it's true? Often, when I taught classes in spirituality, students were looking for the "abnormal" in saints: levitation, bi-location, apparitions, audible voices, miracle-working. Any and all of these phenomena are far from normal, extraordinary to be sure. Perhaps, this is cogent reason for our thinking that a saint is not a normal Christian.

Cardinal Suenens insisted that being holy is exactly what every Christian should ordinarily be. But more than anything else: holiness is a Person, the Holy Spirit. The call of holiness that Vatican II mandates and what we hear from pulpits and in classrooms is the call to the Holy Spirit, the Sanctifier and Creator of all holiness.

As the priest celebrant use to pray in the beginning of Eucharistic Prayer III:

> "All life, all holiness comes from you (Father) through your Son, Jesus Christ our Lord, by the working of the Holy Spirit." The truth still holds!

The Holy Spirit is the holiness of God and makes Christians normal by coming to them to make them saints.

Come, Holy Spirit. Make me a normal Christian; make me a saint.

THE BATTLEFIELD: DEATH VS. LIFE

Whether we like it or not, we are in the midst of a battlefield: life vs. death.

Saint Pope John Paul II spoke about it at the World Youth Day during his homily on the Feast of the Assumption, 15 August 1993, at the Cherry Creek State Park of Denver. He said:

> "A culture of death seeks to impose itself on our desire to live, and to live to the full."

He cited the family especially under attack and the sacred character of human life denied. The weakest members of society are the most at risk: the unborn, children, the sick, the handicapped, the old, the poor, the unemployed, the immigrant and refugee. This was in August 1993; have things changed for the worse or better? You decide.

It was at the farewell ceremony at the former Denver airport that John Paul II mentioned "the culture of life over the culture of death."

> "The culture of life means respect for nature and protection of God's work of creation. In a special way, it means respect for human life from the first moment of conception until its natural end."[100]

On 25 March 1995, Pope John Paul II reiterated the theme in his encyclical *The Gospel of Life:*

> "We are facing an enormous and dramatic clash between good and evil, death and life, the 'culture of death' and the 'culture of life.' We find ourselves not only 'faced with' but necessarily 'in the midst of' this conflict: we are all involved, and we all share in it, with

---

[100] Pope John Paul II, 15 August 1993

the inescapable responsibility of choosing to be unconditionally pro-life."[101]

By the culture of death, we mean injustices, actions, and policies
that dehumanize and frustrate the human striving for fulfillment, but
primarily, forms of unjustifiable homicide, especially abortion and
euthanasia.

Where are you on the battlefield?

Do you change uniforms and switch sides at times?

---

[101] Pope John Paul II encyclical, "The Gospel of Life", #28

PROPHETS

Prophets are people of insight, not foresight. They are meat and potato persons, not gravy or icing. They focus on essentials, top priorities, not the incidentals and superfluous.

Prophets are spokespersons for God, not for themselves. They know their probable destiny for speaking the truth: death.

God sends these prophets to us, these human angels (the word angel means messenger) to remind us what is important in life from God's standpoint, not necessarily ours. The prophets cut to the chase, cut to the heart of the matter, and strive to get us to refocus.

Walk into any bookstore, and there is the section on "Self-improvement." There we find books aimed at making our lives better in some way or other. All we need to do is follow the magic formula step by step, day by day.

The prophets have given the world first things first before any of these modern self-improvement manuals. Look at Elijah and John the Baptizer. They came with flaming words that called us to conversion.

> Then Elijah arose, a prophet like fire, and his word burned like a torch.[102]

> He (John) went into the region around the Jordan, proclaiming a baptism of repentance for the forgiveness of sins.[103]

> John says of Jesus:

> "He will baptize you with the Holy Spirit and fire."[104]

Prophets confront us head-on: our narrowness of heart and mind (how closed are you on either end of the continuum?), our intolerance

---

[102] Sirach 48:1
[103] Luke 3:3
[104] Luke 3:16

(yes, it's there), our narcissism (how much?), prejudices (what/who are they?), impatience (we live in the land of fast everything!), our enslavement to passion (sensuality, sex, pleasure), and undisciplined lives (freedom = license in our society).

CRAZY IN LOVE

You do a lot of crazy things when you are in love. People who forgot what it was like to be madly in love or people who have never been in love, think you are crazy, out of your mind. Maybe you are – certainly out of yourself and thinking about the one you love!

Saint Francis Xavier, the great missionary, wrote Saint Ignatius of Loyola and told him that he thought about going around to the universities of Europe, especially Paris, and crying out like a madman in the classrooms – riveting the attention of those with more learning than charity. Francis Xavier wanted – needed – evangelists for the people had discovered and fell in love with!

How many women and men are crazy in love at this moment? Countless ones!

God is crazy in love with you and me right this minute. The Son of God was born out of love to die out of love for us. God is not only crazy in love with us, but also a jealous lover.

Are you crazy in love with God? With anyone?

MORE PRAYER

After years of praying, after reading and hearing countless talks on prayer, after delivering many presentations on prayer myself, I find that I keep coming back to these points on prayer:

- Prayer is a means and an end.
- It is communication and communion.
- It is a dialogue, not a monologue, and listening.
- It is a conversation with God; sometimes we use words.

Genuine prayer is unceasing, unending. Our life becomes prayer. Saint Teresa of Avila, the expert on prayer, writes:

> "Prayer is not just spending time with God.
> It is partly that – but if it ends there, it is fruitless.
> No, prayer is dynamic.
> Authentic prayer changes us – unmasks us –
> strips us – indicates where growth is needed.
> Authentic prayer never leads us to complacency,
> but needles us – makes us uneasy at times.
> It leads us to true self-knowledge, to true humility."

SAINT VINCENT DE PAUL ON MARY

I was blessed some years ago and spent a month in Paris with a group from the Vincentian Family. It was a great experience because these men and women were from all parts of the world. The speakers were excellent, and I learned much from their wisdom.

One of the presentations was by Father Corpus Delgado, C.M., a Vincentian priest from the Province of Zaragoza, Spain. He focused on Saint Vincent de Paul's attention on three events or mysteries in the life of the Blessed Virgin Mary: The Immaculate Conception, the Annunciation, and the Visitation. As usual, Saint Vincent de Paul was eclectic in his spirituality; he chose what he understood as essential or important and then put his own spin on it. His spirituality is always action-oriented and practical.

The Immaculate Conception:

Saint Vincent saw the young, humble and chaste virgin emptied herself so as to be receptive of God. She allowed herself to be filled with God. Since his Son had to take human flesh through a woman, it was proper that he take it from a woman worthy of receiving him, a woman fully graced, free from sin, filled with piety and far removed from any harmful affection. The Archangel Gabriel approaches Mary: "Greetings, favored one! The Lord is with you."[105]

The Annunciation:

The second movement that St. Vincent discovered in Mary was her knowing her smallness before God, giving herself to God to serve one's neighbor. God gave her the beautiful gift of the Second Person of the Holy Trinity. The Holy Spirit, within her virginal womb, formed a body. God created a soul and united it to this body. The Word united himself

---

[105] Luke 1:28

to this soul and body by a wondrous union. The Holy Spirit wrought the ineffable mystery of the Incarnation.

The Visitation:

Mary visited her cousin Elizabeth. Emptied of herself and given to God, Mary's life is at the service of the poor. Mary goes promptly and cheerfully. She remains there; it was the older woman Elizabeth's first and only child; it was the teenage Mary's first and only child.

These three mysteries in Mary's life speak to us:

- We empty ourselves so that God may fill us up with himself.
- We know our smallness before God.
- We open ourselves to serve our neighbors, especially those who are poor.

THE RICH GUY AND THE BEGGAR

In the Gospel of Saint Luke, chapter 16:19-31, we read the story of the rich man and Lazarus. We can call the rich man "Dives" because it is the Latin term for "rich man."

Dives lives and breathes as his name signifies. He dresses in the latest fashions; he eats better than most; and can afford anything he wants. He apparently displays no compassion for the poor. He is focused on one person: himself.

Lazarus dresses in rags; he knows hunger because he is hungry every day; he struggles to survive. He is too weak to ward off the dogs who lick his open sores.

During their lifetime on earth, there was no chasm between the two men. Lazarus begged outside Dives' gate. Dives probably had to circumvent the man or perhaps one of the servants pushed Lazarus out of the way.

Death comes to both men. Lazarus, a man of deep faith in God, finds himself in the bosom of Abraham. Dives finds himself in *Hades* (Hell).

Now there is a chasm; it is uncrossable and permanent. Dives now realizes its existence.

In hell, Dives makes his pleas for help, to no avail. He had his opportunities.

Some chasms can be crossed or bridged, but not this one.

The story of Dives and Lazarus is a parable of personal relationships. Giving alms to the needy is praiseworthy, but involvement is better. When we give financial assistance to others, we are enriched in the process.

In giving, we receive.

What would have happened to Dives if he had stopped occasionally and helped Lazarus?

What if Dives had given Lazarus a job? That would have solved a root cause of poverty.

COMPLACENCY

The Prophet Amos is one of the good guys. He is the champion of the poor, the prophet of social justice.

God called Amos from a village south of Jerusalem, an ordinary shepherd and dresser of sycamore trees, to be God's spokesperson. And this simple, uneducated man's mission to Israel only lasted a few years, but he left his mark.

Amos took on the social disorders of the upper classes, particularly their heartless luxury and self-indulgence. We see this in the beginning of Amos chapter 6.

The prophet was extremely annoyed with the complacency of these people – their selfish and extravagant use of God's blessings. They spent their entire lives pampering themselves while remaining indifferent to the sufferings of the common ordinary people outside their door and down the street.

Amos' target is the wealthy who secure the best animals designated for sacrifice to the Lord, but which end up on their dinner tables. In Amos' mind, they add sacrilege to their gluttony. He comes on strong!

There is nothing wrong in having a good-size bank account. The issue is those who neglect others through their indifference and complacency.

At the particular judgment, I'm afraid that we will pay for our sins of omissions.

Who is the present Amos of our world?

Who is the champion of social justice?

How complacent are you?

LIFESTYLE OR LIFE?

A few people living in Saint Louis and I had been taking care of Lucas. He was living alone in a room with no running water or electricity in one of the worse slums in Nairobi, Kenya.

I met Lucas while he was in high school. He was the president of the student body and well-accepted by both Catholic and Muslim students in his Catholic boys' high school.

I used to give him shirts and shoes. He slept on the cement floor until I gave him a mattress and a blanket. He depended on paraffin for light at night until I got him a kerosene lamp, but that was stolen.

Lucas had no source of income, and these American friends and I had kept him going. He wanted to go to college (he's very bright) because he saw that it was the only way out of that slum, the only way to a better way of life. I had been paying his tuition, and it had not been easy for me. When I lived in Kenya, I was able to give him shirts and shoes and other items; I don't know how he gets these things now.

During the chaos and turmoil in Kenya after the elections, Lucas had to escape to the parish church and sleep in a pew. When the Red Cross had set up tents in the area, Lucas survived on their assistance. When he tried to sneak back to his room, he was beat up by the rebels and the police.

You and I have a lifestyle; Lucas had a life, although, at times, he wondered. He has sometimes gone for three days or more without food. He has been locked out of his meager room when I didn't get rent over to him fast enough; the landlord was/is intolerant.

What kind of life is this? But the fact is, it is his life and the life of too many like Lucas.

Sometimes we gripe about our lifestyle and wish that it were better.

Why are we dissatisfied with our lifestyle? Or are we?

Do we have a lifestyle or a life?

THE GOOD SAMARITAN

My dear friend, Greg Jewell, a Catholic married layperson, a Franciscan, and I left the city of Jerusalem for Jericho. It was morning, and we had to deal with traffic, except this day it was worse. Some Jewish people were protesting the government and so they decided to set fire to large truck tires at major intersections. Because of billows of black smoke and traffic snarls, we had to make various detours.

The Franciscan was driving the car. My friend was in the front seat and I had the back seat for myself. The two in the front were talking up a storm. I noticed that the temperature gage on the dashboard was indicating that the engine was getting hot – and hotter. It was moving into the red area of the gage.

I yelled out: "Look at the temperature gage!" And the friar slowed down and turned into a side road. In God's providence, we were at the site of the *Inn of the Good Samaritan*!

The smoke was pouring out of the radiator. We got out of the car, and as was our custom, I read the gospel which, in this case, was that of the Good Samaritan.

To the right of the car, was a large Bedouin tent. At a distance in front of us was a small building with a chained German Shepherd who wanted to come and chew us up. He was doing everything he could to break that chain. Out of the tent came two young Arabs. They quickly sized up the situation. One of the men went back into the tent, the other went toward the barking dog to fetch water.

The one Arab immediately started to pour water into the radiator to cool down the engine; the other Arab came out of the tent carrying a silver tray with large shot glasses of hot tea. We toasted each other. After more water, the engine cooled down.

My friend offered the Arabs a twenty-dollar bill, but they refused to take it. He insisted; finally, they took it. And we drove off.

As we drove back to Jerusalem to switch cars, my friend and I talked about the hospitality showed to us by these two Arabs. They saved us.

Have you been a good Samaritan lately?

May I suggest that you read Luke 10:25-37?

THE JERICHO ROAD

The road from Jerusalem to Jericho runs approximately twenty miles, not very far, but within the short mileage, it drops from 2600 feet above sea level to 550 feet below sea level.

Jericho is a city of palm trees and beautiful fruit orchards.

During the time of Jesus, the road was known for its robbers. It was a dangerous twenty miles for anyone especially if traveling alone.

We know the story of the Good Samaritan who stops and cares for a Jewish traveler who is robbed and left half-dead on the Jericho road. It is the story of goodness overriding prejudice.

Martin Luther King Jr. speaks about the Jericho Road:

> "A true revolution of values will soon cause us to question the fairness and justice of many of our past and present policies. We are called to play the Good Samaritan on life's roadside, but that will be only an initial act. One day we must come to see that the whole Jericho road must be transformed so that men and women will not be constantly beaten and robbed as they make their journey on life's highway. True compassion is more than flinging a coin to a beggar... compassion sees that an edifice that produces beggars needs restructuring. A true revolution of values will soon look uneasily on the glaring contrast of poverty and wealth."

How do those words of Martin Luther King Jr. strike you? Are you a true compassionate person?

SAINT JOSEPH

A painting that caught my attention was one by the famous artist Pietro Annigoni who died in 1988. He did portraits of popes, US presidents, the British royalty, and many others.

Annigoni painted a picture of Joseph and Jesus at the carpenter's table. Joseph looks like a mixture of a black African and some other race. He is strong and hefty. Jesus has blond hair and looks like a youngster from a Scandinavian country or perhaps northern Italy.

I found the characterizations and the gestures most interesting.

No one lived in such intimacy with Mary as Joseph did. Although legally married, they both lived chaste celibacy. From a pure human standpoint, this had to be most difficult for both of them, especially when each of them was such a loving and lovable person. To live chaste celibacy with a man or woman 24/7, year after year had to take heroic virtue. Yes, there are married people who live such lives deliberately, but it is most often because of serious physical and/or marital problems.

Scripture tells us that Joseph was a just man. This means that he was a man of integrity, a man of loyalty, and a man of fidelity. We see this justice played out in his care for his wife, Mary, and foster-child, Jesus.

God communicated to Joseph three times that we know of, not through apparitions, but through dreams, and Joseph responded to each dream.

Joseph was obedient to what was revealed to him. He listened and responded. (To *obey* in Latin means "to listen"). I think that Joseph's hallmark is obedience.

One of my favorite holy cards is Joseph taking care of the infant Jesus in the middle of the night while Mary is sleeping in the background. Can you not picture Joseph holding and talking to the child Jesus?

Another holy card that I like is Joseph teaching the young Jesus some tricks of the trade in his carpentry workshop.

Saint Joseph is the patron of the universal church.

Saint Joseph is the patron of a happy death.

He is the patron of carpenters, of nations, and of dioceses.

He is the patron of many who bear his name.

Saint Joseph, pray for us now and at the hour of our death. Amen.

BROTHERS

Our Vincentian community here at St. Mary's of the Barrens consists of priests and brothers.

What is a brother, you might ask? A Brother is a man who is a member of a religious order or institute but who is neither ordained nor studying for the priesthood. He professes vows of poverty, celibate chastity, and obedience.[106] Our Vincentian Brothers also take the vow of stability.

Since taking up residency here, we have had four of our brothers pass on to eternal life. I am thinking at the moments of Brothers John, Tom, Richard, and Leo. These men held various ministries and were men of great faith and Vincentian spirituality. I miss them, their example, and assistance!

In his lifetime, the founder of our community, St. Vincent de Paul, relied on the talents of a number of brothers. His secretaries, Bertrand and Louis, that handled his correspondence were brothers. He used brothers such as Jean to assist in staffing French consuls and to reach out to those held captive by pirates in the Tunis and Algiers. Vincent had two particular brothers, Mathieu (aka The Fox) and Jean Parre, that would run money through the war zone in France to help the injured and homeless and to bring people to a safe haven. Brother Alexandre was in charge of the pharmacy and infirmary at the motherhouse in Paris.

Today, our community is blessed in having other talented brothers that help further the work of the church.

Perhaps you have a brother as a sibling whom you admire. When was the last time you spoke? Unfortunately, my brother Bill was the first of my siblings to enter eternal life. I pray for him often.

Do you have brothers?

---

[106] Religious Brother.org, What Words Mean

APP

I recently lived in a college seminary; by that I mean, the seminarians attended a near-by university. One thing about them is that they are hi-tech individuals. They know computers, mobile phones, iPads, etc.

I often relied on one of them for help. Recently, I had a computer problem which completely mystified me. One of the seminarians, an ex-military man who had worked with computers, came to my rescue, and not only corrected the problem but showed me how to improve my machine.

App – there is an app for everything. *App* is short for "applications" that you may download to your phone, iPad, chrome book, or whatever to do all sorts of things.

There are "God Tools" and other God apps. Others are related to prayer and the Bible. My eye doctor showed me his latest app: all the Sunday readings from sacred scripture. He told me that he took his iPad to church every Sunday.

Apps are fine and helpful, but you can't find one that enables you to love more compassionately or relieve the suffering of another human being.

Apps offer you the chance to play God in a game – to equate God with power. For example, being God means you can make others do what you want. You can zap the driver of a car that cuts in front of you and cause his four tires to go flat.

But there is a God app that is free, and you don't need an app store to get it downloaded.

The God app is love. And it is indeed free.

Remember "grace"? It is a gift freely given for the asking.

MURDERED FOR GOD

In the beginning of every year, the Vatican releases the number of missionaries killed during the previous year. It seems to me that the number is increasing.

I was pastor of a church in Denver, Colorado. One of the former pastors, a Franciscan, was murdered while giving out Holy Communion at Mass. I often thought of him when I was distributing Holy Communion in that same church.

Two priests with whom I associated in Kenya were both murdered. Father Martin Addai, a Missionary of Africa, from Ghana, was shot dead in his car as he was leaving the seminary grounds. He was 41 years old and taught medical moral at Tangaza College. We would see each other every month at formators' meetings.

Another priest who was killed was Father Guiseppe Bertaina, a Consolata Missionary. He was originally from Italy and had given his life to the African missions. He was tied up and gagged by robbers. The priest suffocated to death by the excessive material in his mouth.

I think of these men. And thank God for their service to the church.

Pray for those men and women who are giving their lives as missionaries around the world. Not all are religious or ordained; there are a good number of laypersons who are dying for the faith, and some are martyrs in the formal sense.

DIED FOR GOD

We can't forget all those who died by reason of the coronavirus crisis. Priests, religious men and women, those who had insisted on reaching out to people in need.

We can't forget the medical personnel who died caring for the inflicted.

God have mercy on their souls.

SAINT LOUISE AND SAINT VINCENT DE PAUL

Behind every great man there is a great woman and that includes great saints. In the case of Saint Vincent de Paul it was Saint Louise de Marillac.

They had a long relationship. He was man; she was woman. She was a wife and a mother. He was a priest; she was a lay woman. He was 10 years older than she. He was, at the time they met, in fairly good health; she was not in the greatest of health.

Louise was from nobility and illegitimate. Vincent was from a rural farming background in southwestern France. Louise was trained by Dominican nuns. Her education, intelligence, and Catholicism led her to God, and God led her to the poor. Vincent's intelligence, character, temperament, and personal background led him to the poor.

Vincent had a degree in theology, but, in my mind, Louise was the theologian. Louise was transparent; Vincent was opaque as far as his inner spiritual life was concerned. We read of her deep insights, the fruit of her prayer. Louise had a devotion to the sacred humanity of Jesus which led her to deep contemplation. Vincent's spirituality was eclectic, and he was more an active contemplative.

From Ascension Thursday, 25 May, to Pentecost, 4 June 1623, Louise was in great desolation. She did not know what to do. Should she leave her husband to serve God and others? Find another spiritual director because she was too dependent on him?...She worried about the immortality of her soul.

On Pentecost Sunday, 4 June 1623, in the Church of Saint Nicholas-des-Champs, Paris, everything was clarified for her in what she called her *Lumiere*. The Holy Spirit answered her three concerns.

Vincent de Paul became Louise's spiritual director and held the role for 38 years. The relationship developed into collaboration and a deep friendship. I think that Louise was Vincent's closest friend among many other relationships.

Louise died in March 1660. Vincent would follow her in September of the same year.

Vincent gave two conferences to the Daughters of Charity whom Louise and he had co-founded. In these talks, he expressed his true feelings for her and revealed something of her great spirituality.

Can a single man and a widow maintain a long, chaste celibate relationship?

The answer is yes. Look at Saints Vincent and Louise.

JEALOUSY OR ENVY?

They are different you know, but we have fallen into the trap of using jealousy and envy interchangeably, although there is a difference.

When I am jealous of you, you have something I want, and I want to have it inordinately. You have something good or there is something good about you, and I want to have it. The emphasis is on "I want it".

Envy is anger or sadness at the goodness or excellence of someone else because I see it is lessening my own status. But the key difference between jealousy and envy is with envy, I don't want to possess the good or whatever you have. I want to destroy it.

As I get older, I see how sins can be more subtle. Envy is not always obvious. It can be very subtle. When someone we know gets a promotion or a big raise, we may start doing a number on her – and try to kill her reputation. Why? To make ourselves feel better about ourselves. This is bulls-eye envy!

Saint Augustine calls envy "the diabolical sin." Because from envy are born such evils as hatred, detraction, calumny, joy caused by the misfortunate of a neighbor, and displeasure caused by his prosperity.

Are you jealous or envious?

Which one?

EYES

In the Christian tradition, Saint Lucy is the patron of the blind and Saint Odilia patron of those with eye problems.

When I think of Saint Lucy, I think of Margaret O'Malley. Margaret had worked for years in the public-school system of Chicago and was an active parishioner in our parish. What many people did not know was that Margaret was a consecrated lay woman.

One day Margaret asked me to pray over her eyes; she was going blind. She asked me also if I could buy her a small statue of Saint Lucy which I did. Anytime I entered her home, there in the parlor on the shelf over the fireplace was Saint Lucy. Whenever I visited Margaret and brought her Holy Communion, she asked me to pray over her eyes. Margaret lost her vision before she died.

Saint Lucy's name means "light." We don't know too much about her except that she lived in Syracuse, Sicily and was martyred under Diocletian. Legend has it that the Roman Emperor had her eyes put out as part of her torture. In his grace, God restored Lucy's eyes. That's why, many times in statues of Lucy, she is seen holding a dish with two eyes on it.

I lost sight in my left eye, and I know first-hand how precious our vision is. God, in his infinite wisdom, gave us two eyes. I now depend totally on my right eye.

My friend, Clarence introduced me to Saint Odilia, a French woman of the seventh century who was born blind. Catholic tradition tells us that Odilia was baptized at twelve years old and as the priest anointed her with the oil of chrism, her blindness was cured. Through the generosity of her father, Odilia was given a castle to use as a convent from which she served the poor and needy.

The two things that Lucy and Odilia have in common: they are patrons of those with eye problems and both celebrate their feast day on December 13.

I recommend to anyone with eye problems to pray to either Saint Lucy or Saint Odilia – or both.

Many people have physical sight but are spiritually blind.

CAFETERIA CHRISTIANITY AND HOT TUB RELIGION

These expressions, *Cafeteria Christianity* and *Hot Tub Religion* are derogatory terms. I have heard them more often from televangelists than from Catholic pulpits, although I have used the expression Cafeteria Catholics more than once.

The idea behind cafeteria Christians is the choice of doctrine they will follow and those they will not. It is a pick-and-choose of religious beliefs. I heard one well-known televangelist say that "Cafeteria Christianity is today's theology."

This implies subjective selectivity and differences of opinion according to one's own whims and fancies.

Hot Tub Religion has been related to hedonism or the theology of enjoyment.

James Innell Packer in *Laid-Back Religion* criticizes "hot tub religion." He says that hot tub religion attempts to harness the power of God to the priorities of self-centeredness.

> "Hot tub religion is Christianity corrupted by the passion
> of pleasure…symptoms include overheated supernatu-
> ralism that seeks signs, wonders, visions, prophecies,
> and miracles…constant soothing syrup from electronic
> preachers and the liberal pulpit…anti-intellectual senti-
> mentalism and emotional 'highs' deliberately cultivated,
> the Christian equivalent of cannabis and coca.[107]

Where are you: in the cafeteria line waiting to make your choices?
Or do you always choose the "right" things?
What's going on in the hot tub?

---

[107] Laid-Back Religion, 1989: p.53,58

CANCER

Bishop John T. Steinbock, Diocese of Fresno, California died of cancer 5 December 2010. Before he died, he wrote *An Essay on a Christian Perspective: The Affliction of Cancer.*

Bishop Steinbock wrote this essay 1 October 2010, but he also wrote a pastoral message November 2010. I recommend both for anyone suffering from cancer or who is involved with someone diagnosed with cancer.

In the essay, Bishop Steinbock offers a list of ten blessings for those who struggle with cancer. They are for reflection:

1. We come to know how much so many care for us and love us.
2. We grow in humility, allowing other people to care for us when we are most sick.
3. We are led to greater prayer in our life, realizing our need for the Lord and our absolute dependence on him.
4. We come to reflect on the blessings we have received throughout our lives.
5. We are able to be united even more in the suffering of Christ.
6. We are able to make atonement for our own personal sins and for the sins of those we love.
7. We are able to give witness to the Lord Jesus.
8. Our suffering unites us to everyone in the human race.
9. We come to appreciate the great gift of science and of medicine and the gift of those who care for us.
10. Added thoughts:
    We come to realize that our spiritual life is more important than physical life.
    Give thanks to God each day for another day in our lives.
    The joy of being alive another day.
    Begin to realize what life is all about: eternal life and our own mortality.

Since I have written this piece, I have come down with prostate cancer. Now I know something of what the infliction is....

ANAWIM OF TODAY

God never, ever reneges on his promises. He promised that there would be a faithful remnant left in Israel after the defeat of the country by alien military forces. And there was!

We read about the anawim – the remnant. They play a major role in the Old and New Testament. I remember studying about these people in scripture classes.

Who are the anawim of today? They are the humble, devoid of arrogance and pride. They are the simple, common folk. The word *anaw* or *ani* will come to represent those who opt to live lives of material simplicity for the sake of others. These would be those women and men of today who live out the vow of poverty.

They are not necessarily the destitute, but those who voluntarily have little and are open to receive everything from God. They are people of integrity. They are the people of fidelity.

Saint Pope John Paul II speaks of the anawim:

> "It indicates not just the oppressed, the miserable, the persecuted for justice, but also those who, with fidelity to the moral teaching of the Alliance with God, are marginalized by those who prefer to use violence, riches, and power. In this light one understands that the category of the 'poor' is not just a social category but a spiritual choice. It is what the famous Beatitude means: 'Blessed are the poor in spirit, for theirs is the Kingdom of heaven' (Mt 5:3). The prophet Zephaniah spoke to the anawim as special persons: 'Seek the Lord, all you humble of the land, who do his commands; seek righteousness, seek humility; perhaps you may be hidden on the day of wrath of the Lord.'" (Zep 2:3).[108]

---

[108] General Audience. Wednesday, 23 May 2001

Pope Benedict XVI gave a commentary on Mary's Magnificat:

"It is a canticle that reveals the spirituality of the biblical anawim, that is, of those faithful who not only recognize themselves as 'poor' in the detachment from all idolatry of riches and power, but also in the profound humility of heart emptied of the temptation to pride and open to the bursting in of the divine saving grace. Indeed, the whole Magnificat…is marked by this 'humility', in Greek 'tapeinosis', which indicates a situation of material humility and poverty."[109]

Do you dare to classify yourself as a anawim?
If not, then who?

---

[109] General Audience, 15 February 2006

SACRED EXCHANGE

We are indebted to Leo Tolstoy for this story:

> A rather severe monarch requested that his priests and
> sages show him God so that he might see him. Of course,
> the magi were not able to fulfill his desire. A shepherd
> volunteered to take on the task. He told the king that his
> eyes were not good enough to see God.
>
> The king then shifted his request: "I want to know at
> least what God does."
> In his boldness, the shepherd told the king, "We must
> exchange our clothes."
>
> This made the king pause, yet out of curiosity if nothing
> else, about the answers that he expected from the shep-
> herd, he agreed. The king gave the shepherd his royal
> garments and he dressed himself in the simple clothes
> of the poor man.
>
> Then came the answer. This is what God does!

This is what the Son of God has done. The Son of God shed his divine
splendor.
Saint Paul says it clearly:

> "He emptied himself, taking the form of a slave, being
> born in human likeness.
> And being found in human form, he humbled himself
> and became obedient to the point of death – even death
> on the cross."[110]

---

[110] Philippians 2:7-8

The Early Fathers of the Church called this "the sacred exchange." God took on what was ours, so that we might receive what was his and become like to God. Saint Augustine boldly says that God became man so that man might become God.

As the priest says quietly at the preparation of the gifts:

> *By the mystery of this water and wine may we come to share in the divinity of Christ, who humbled himself to share in our humanity.*

This is what happens on our baptism day. There is a sacred exchange. We are clothed with the white baptismal garment. We receive forgiveness of original sin and all personal sins, birth into the new life by which we become an adoptive child of the Father, a member of Christ and a temple of the Holy Spirit, incorporated into the Church, and made a sharer in the priesthood of Christ.[111]

---

[111] CCC # 1279

A LITERAL LOOK

"Are you envious because I am generous?"[112] The original text literally translates: *Is your eye evil because I am good?* For us in the 21st century, this sounds quite mysterious...*Is your eye evil because I am good?*

In the prior text to this verse, we read that workers who borne the heat and burden of the day are not thrilled at all by the generosity of their employer. They resented his generosity to the late comers – the fact that every worker got the same salary. I don't think that union personnel would like it either!

Were their eyes evil because he was good?

I am reminded of the *Ojo de* Dios – (The eye of God) – I used to have hanging in my office years ago. Was the Ojo de Dios watching me or anyone else who had an Ojo de Dios hanging in their homes? We certainly can't classify Ojo de Dios as an evil eye.

I found out that the Ojo de Dios is an ancient symbol made by the Huichol Indians of northwestern Mexico and the Aymara Indians of Bolivia.

The *Ojo* is symbolic of seeing and understanding the unknown and unknowable. The Mystery. The four points of the woven Ojo represent the earth, fire, air, and water, the four elements.

In Mexico, the Ojo de Dios was made when a child was born. Each year, a bit of yarn was added until the child turned five at which point the Ojo de Dios was complete.

In Bolivia, the Ojo de Dios was made to be placed on an altar so that the gods could watch over the praying people and protect them

In the ancient Middle East and still today in some locations, people have thought that the eye of an envious person actually becomes in some sense actively evil, capable of doing some type of harm to those under the gaze of a person's envious eye. Is this pure superstition?

A person who is envious may act it out and steal from someone or do a person some degree of harm.

---

[112] Matthew 20:15

Envy can lead us to the evil eye of resentment. The generosity of God far outstrips our sense of fairness – of equality. What we need to understand in head and heart is…all is grace.

Are we envious because God is generous?

THE CHURCH AND MARY

If I may, I would like to recommend the writings of Blessed Isaac of Stella. They are quite accessible.

Isaac was born in England around1100 AD, educated in England and Paris, and joined the Cistercian community of Citeaux, near Dijon. He was a contemporary of Saint Bernard of Clairvaux. Isaac became abbot of the Cistercian monastery of Stella where he gained a reputation for his holiness of life and teaching. He died in 1169 AD.

This is an excerpt from one of his sermons:

> "In the inspired Scriptures,
> what is said in a universal sense of the virgin mother,
> the Church,
> is understood in an individual sense of the Virgin Mary,
> and what is said in a particular sense of the virgin
> mother Mary
> is rightly understood in a general sense of the virgin
> mother, the Church.
> When either is spoken of, the meaning can be under-
> stood of both,
> almost without qualification.
>
> In a way, every Christian is also believed to be a bride
> of God's Word,
> a mother of Christ, his daughter and sister, at once vir-
> ginal and fruitful.
> These words are used in a universal sense of the Church,
> in a special sense of Mary,
> in a particular sense of the individual Christian.
> They are used by God's Wisdom in person,
> the Word of the Father."[113]

How do you see the relationship between Mary and the Church?

---

[113] Sermo 51PPL 194, 1862-1863, 1865

TWO BROTHERS: YES AND NO

Jesus asks of the religious authorities their opinion, something he rarely did. He presents a parable of two brothers in Matthew 21:28-32.

> Two sons are asked by their father to work in the vineyard.
> The first son says flat out: "No," but he changes his mind, and goes.
> The second son says: "Yes," but does not do it.
> Here is where their opinion comes in: "Which of the brothers did the will of their father?"

These religious leaders and others refused to believe in the teaching and preaching of John the Baptizer, and, of course, Jesus himself. On the other hand, who did believe in John? The tax collectors and prostitutes, those people who were regarded as grievously sinful individuals...THEY believed. These men and women heard John's call to repentance and acted upon it. The leaders rejected John and Jesus after him in spite of the large crowds who listened to him and followed him.

The religious authorities were like the son who said yes but did not follow through. They were experts in the Lord's word, but not necessarily doers of it.

If I may play the role of a defense attorney: sometimes our first response is not always the best, especially in times of crisis. Our actions, however, show what and who we are.

Jesus has given us the prime example of someone who accepted God's will 24/7.

Where do you stand?

A yes or no sister or brother?

LOVE IS TWO-SIDED

When various saints speak of love, they speak about it under two aspects: affective and effective love.

Affective love: a kind of overflowing of the person who loves into the person who is loved or a feeling of tenderness for one loved, such as our mother has for us her children.

Affective love speaks to our emotions – the love that we feel for God, for others, for ourselves, within our heart.

Effective love: doing those things which the person loved wants or desires or commands. This is the kind of love Jesus speaks of: "If anyone loves me, he will keep my commandments."

Effective love is something we do, a positive action for the good of another.

The word *misericordia* literally means "having a merciful heart" both affectively and effectively. Miseri + cordia – mercy + heart.

As we used to say in the Marriage Encounter movement, love is a decision, not an emotion. Love is an act of the will. I choose to love you. As married couples know, as single lovers know, as consecrated religious or ordained know, sometimes you don't feel like loving, but you choose to love. You decide then and there to love.

What about your affective love?

What about your effective love?

HOT CROSS BUNS AND PRETZELS

Thank you, Lent, for two favorite foods: hot cross buns and pretzels!

I remember as a youngster going to *Weiss' Bakery* on Fullerton Avenue, Chicago, for hot cross buns. Although these buns were baked primarily for Good Friday, they have become "sweet rolls" for Lent and, in some places, for other times of the year.

Tradition tells us that Father Tomas Rockliffe of Saint Alban's Abbey, England, developed the original recipe for these buns in 1361. The monks gave them out to the poor who came looking for something to eat on Good Friday. The distinctive feature of the hot cross buns was the cross cut into the top of each bun and white icing piped in after baking.

Hot cross buns were a clever visual aid for Good Friday.

History tells us that during Queen Elizabeth I's reign, when Roman Catholicism was prohibited, the faithful were tried for Popery for signing the cross on their Good Friday buns. The popularity of the buns increased, so the Queen passed a law which limited the making of hot cross buns to certain religious times, e.g., Christmas, Easter, or funerals.

Again, thanks to an Italian monk in northern Italy, we have the pretzel. Because fat, eggs, and milk were forbidden, the monk baker made bread out of flour, water, and salt. He did not want to waste the left-over dough, so he rolled it into ropes and twisted each rope into a three-part loop. The three holes symbolized the Holy Trinity: Father, Son, and Holy Spirit. The twisted center resembled how the monks prayed: arms folded across their chest.

As the English monks gave out hot cross buns to the poor on Good Friday, these Italian monks gave out the crisp breads to local children as a reward for memorizing their prayers. They called the breads *braciola* which in Latin means "little arms." Other monasteries picked up the idea from the original baker and braciola spread into Germany where it became known as *brezel*, in English "pretzel".

Do you like hot cross buns and pretzels?

We owe the monks a big thank you!

PYGMALION

Pygmalion is a Greek name. It may refer to a man in ancient Greek mythology, a sculptor who fell in love with his statue that he had carved. Or, Pygmalion may refer to a character in Virgil's poem, *Aeneid* which our college seminarians know from class readings.

I prefer to think that it was the Greek sculptor that George Bernard Shaw had in mind when he wrote his stage play in 1912.

Many are familiar with the Broadway musical and subsequent film *My Fair Lady*. Here, phonetics Professor Higgins very definitely falls in love with his creation, Eliza Doolittle.

Shaw's play, as well as the musical and film version narrate Professor Higgins' challenge that he can transform a low-class cockney woman into a charming socialite simply by teaching her proper etiquette and pronunciation. And he does it! *The Rain in Spain Stays Mainly in the Plains*...a great musical number by Frederick Lowe and Alan Jay Lerner.

Do you ever see yourselves as Pygmalion?

Do you see God's desire to transform your lives?

Do you see God as a type of "Professor Higgins" who never forces you to do anything, but who wants you to change yourselves – to shed your dreadful etiquette (your immoral behavior) and cooperate with his grace?

OZ

I watched the *Wizard of Oz* again recently. How many times have I seen this classic? "Oz" brings back a lot of memories. I remember walking down Webster Avenue when Oz Park in Chicago was nothing but empty lots covered with broken bricks and debris. It was a definite eyesore for a long time. Oz Park was completed in 1976 and named in honor of Lyman Frank Baum, the author of *The Wonderful Wizard of Oz.*

Now the park has statues of Dorothy and Toto, the Tin Man, Scarecrow, and the Cowardly Lion. The thirteen-acre park is a beautiful addition to the neighborhood.

We look upon The Wizard of Oz as a fairy tale, a delightful story, but others read much more into it. The book has been dissected and analyzed for years. Many see it as a political commentary of the times (Baum wrote it in 1900). Others read Christian themes in the story.

Whatever is the true meaning -- and Baum refused to give an official interpretation -- we can see definite Christian themes that may be helpful.

Every character in Oz conveys a deeper meaning than what is seen on the surface.

Dorothy wants to go home.

The scarecrow wants brains.

The tin man wants a heart.

The lion wants courage.

Each one discovers that what they wanted was never really lost; they had it all along.

What about us Christians?

How often do we uncover, not recover, within us what we thought was not there?

Do we not forget about Emmanuel, God with us?

Let's follow the yellow brick road, not to any wizard, but to Jesus Christ.

LACORDAIRE'S PRAYER

A tradition in many seminaries is that the ordinand class has a prayer card printed for enclosure in their ordination invitations. Many ordinands also have these cards available at their first Masses.

A popular prayer during my time in seminary formation was Father Henri-Dominique Lacordaire's prayer for priests.

> To live in the midst of the world
> with no desire for its pleasure...
> to be a member of every family yet belonging to none...
> to share all suffering,
> to penetrate all secrets,
> to heal all wounds...
> to daily go from men to God to offer him their petitions...
> to return from God to men to offer them his hope...
> to have a heart of fire for charity
>   and a heart of bronze for chastity...
> to bless and be blest forever,
> O God, what a life
> and it is yours, O priest of Jesus Christ!

I invite you to pray for your pastor and parish priests!

BAPTISM OF JESUS

Jesus joins the queue of those wanting John's baptism. It is not what we know as baptism or christening, but a water ritual performed by John the Baptizer in the Jordan River. The water externalized what the recipient internalized or wanted: a change of mind and heart. It was not a sacrament.

Jesus' step into the water was the initial act of his public ministry. He had lived a hidden life for some thirty years, now he was going public. He was entering the public arena.

What a radical change in lifestyle! He moves from an introvert-activity to extrovert-activity, from small village to global village, from carpenter to teacher, preacher, evangelist.

Jesus' "baptism" was an act of identification: Jesus was identifying himself with the people he came to save: sinners of the world.

"We have one who in every respect has been tested as we are, yet without sin."[114]

He sought out the baptism. His action served as a model of service for what he would be doing until his death: he placed himself smack-dab in the middle of humanity. He saw himself as one who serves, not to be served.

He was motivated by mission, the mission of his heavenly Father. He was missionary of the Father.

Your baptism entered you into the public area of the Church. You too are now a missionary.

> "The Church is missionary by nature and her principal task is evangelization, which aims to proclaim and to witness to Christ and to promote his Gospel of peace and love in every environment and culture."[115]

---

[114] Heb. 4:15-16
[115] Pope Benedict XVI, Address to PARTICIPANTS IN THE Fifth International Congress of Military Ordinariates, 26 October 2006

LET'S TAKE A LOOK AT THE MANGER SCENE

Do you see what I see?

I see shepherds, the outcasts of their societal system – illiterate, un-educated, marginalized, the bottom rung of the ladder.

I see animals – cattle, sheep, and a donkey (the one Mary rode to Bethlehem). After all it is a manger; it's their home. Their presence brings a degree of warmth into the cold night and early morning air.

I see kings – three, maybe – who bring adult gifts, not gifts fit for a new-born baby. Those of you who attend baby showers know what to bring a baby!

These men are at the top rung of the ladder. The Magi – the wise, the educated, Gentiles, pagans.

I see Mary and Joseph, exhausted from a long journey, especially Mary… nine months pregnant after having ridden on a donkey for miles on rocky and uneven roads and paths! How did she do that? And both, rejected by Inn keepers, now find their home in a cave with animals. Mary and Joseph were not angelic beings, but what human beings were and are meant to be.

Jesus – the vulnerable, helpless, God become man out of infinite love. The infant Jesus is completely dependent on his mother for milk, warmth, hygiene, comfort, changing his diapers, and burping him.

Do you see what I see?

Are there others to add to the scene?

How dependent are you on Jesus?

ROI

You in the business world know what ROI stands for: *Return on Investment.*

I celebrated a Mass for Legatus and talked on ROI because it fit the gospel: Matthew 10:7-15.

Jesus sends the apostles out in pairs and tells them to take no money, no back-pack, no change of clothes, go bare-footed, and use no walking stick. And then adds: stay at anyone's home that will take you in.

Is Jesus a shrewd businessperson or what?

His instructions meant no transportation costs, no food expense, no hotel bills, and no worry about luggage. Does this not promise a fabulous ROI?

Remember also: Jesus paid no salaries and gave no perks.

Again, a great ROI!

His sale's force dealt in spirituality, not material goods.

His product: The Kingdom of Heaven has come near. Cure the sick, raise the dead, cleanse the lepers, cast out demons.

You received without payment; give without payment.

EPIPHANY

The word *epiphany* in Greek means "manifestation" or "striking appearance."

In today's jargon, I hear the word used more often than ever before. "Did you have an epiphany?" "She had a profound epiphany last month."

Traditionally in the church, the Feast of the Epiphany celebrates three manifestations of God in Christ: to the Magi; at the baptism in the Jordan River; and at the village of Cana. At one time in our liturgy, we separated these manifestations and celebrated them with their own liturgies.

Saint Odilo of Cluny writes:

> "To offer gold is to proclaim Christ's kingship,
> to offer incense is to adore his Godhead,
> and to offer myrrh is to acknowledge his mortality."

What has been your experience?
Can you pinpoint "epiphanies" in your life?
How has God manifested himself to you?

OUR STOOPING GOD

Saint Paul talks about the Son of God emptying himself and taking the form of a slave. Paul gives us a presentation of humility on the part of God.

When I reflect on the mystery of Christmas and of the Incarnation, I see them as the "stooping of God."

Recently I saw a detailed explanation of how a star could have guided the Magi to Bethlehem. How immense is our universe – or is the word infinite more accurate? The God who made this universe chose to become human – born as a helpless infant from the womb of a fourteen or fifteen-year-old Jewish girl. God stooped.

God stooped time and again in dealing with us. He stooped at the Last Supper and washed and dried the feet of the apostles. He stooped and was nailed to the cross and died for our sins.

Catherine de Hueck Doherty said that priests are to be men of towel and basin.

Are not we all?

We all need to stoop for God.

THE HOLY NAME

How often, as a youngster, I heard that our parish's Holy Name Society would be receiving Communion next Sunday – or that the Holy Name Society was having a breakfast after an early Sunday Mass.

The society seemed to be a strong group dedicated to the promotion of devotion to the Holy Name of Jesus and mutual assistance in the attainment of holiness of life. Today, the society is composed of groups across the United States, Canada, Puerto Rico, and the Philippines.

On 3 January of every New Year, the church commemorates the Feast of the Holy Name of Jesus. It is a good way to start a new year. We honor the Mother of God on 1 January, and she, as usual, points immediately to her Son, Jesus.

In Aramaic, *Jesus* is "Yeshua." Parents are the ones that ordinarily name their child, but not in the case of Jesus. The Archangel Gabriel, sent from God, named the child:

> And now, you will conceive in your womb and bear a son, and you will name him Jesus.[116]

Jesus: the name signifies his mission: The Son of God became human in order to save and redeem humankind.

Jesus' precursor, Saint John the Baptist, proclaims Jesus as "the Lamb of God who takes away the sin of the world!"[117]

Saint Paul writes:

> "Therefore, God also highly exalted him and gave him the name that is above every name, so that at the name of Jesus every knee should bend, in heaven and on earth and under the earth, and every tongue should confess that Jesus Christ is Lord, to the glory of God the Father."[118]

---

[116] Luke 1:31
[117] John 1:29
[118] Philippians 2:9-11

We proclaim Jesus' name as holy, and it is, but how many times a day is it used in any way but holy?

How many times is it used in cursing, profanity, and blasphemy?

People make a lot of resolutions, a good one would be to watch the use of the Holy Name of Jesus.

CRITICISM OF THE CHURCH

There is plenty of criticism of the Catholic Church today from both ends of the spectrum. The beginning point is the hierarchy. Are they guilty of sins of commission and omission? Oh, yes! Is anyone capable of throwing the first stone? In today's world, I have the feeling that we could quickly form a queue.

Where do we begin to eliminate the criticism? Who goes first? What goes first? Then second, then third, etc.

The church is a living organism. It is not a lifeless entity. Look at its 2000 years of history!

The words of the late Carlo Caretto are good ones to ponder for many of us:

> "How much I must criticize you, my Church, and yet how much I love you!
> You have made me suffer more than anyone, yet I owe more to you than to anyone. I should like to see you destroyed, and yet I need your presence.
> You have given me much scandal, my Church,
> and yet you alone have made me understand holiness.
> Never in this world have I seen anything more compromised, falser,
> yet never have I touched anything purer, more generous, or more beautiful.
> Countless time I have felt like leaving you, my Church.
> And yet every night I have prayed that I might die in your warm loving arms."[119]

What are your sentiments toward the church or your parish community?

---

[119] Carlo Carreto, The God Who Comes

TU SCENDI DALLE STELLE

Tu Scendi Dalle Stelle (You Come Down from the Stars). I was delighted to see Andrea Bocelli sing this carol on a Christmas special with David Foster. It is a favorite of our Italian brothers and sisters throughout the world.

Many people know specific things about Saint Alphonsus Liguori: he was founder of the Redemptorist family, a civil and canon lawyer, a renown moral theologian, was consecrated a bishop by Pope Clement XIII, and the list goes on. But most people do not know that Alphonsus wrote approximately fifty religious songs.

In December 1744, he composed the Christmas song: *Tu scendi dalle stelle* in time for Christmas services.

There are several English translations; I would like to attempt mine (literal).

You come down from the stars
Oh, king of heaven
And come in a cave
In the cold, in the frost
And come in a cave
In the cold, in the frost.

Oh, my divine Baby
I see you trembling
Oh, Blessed God
Ah, how much it cost you
You loving me
Ah, how much it cost you
You loving me.

For you who are of the world
The Creator
No robes and fire
Oh my Lord

No robes and fire
Oh my Lord.

Dear chosen, little infant
This direst poverty
Makes me love you more
Since love made you
Poor now
Since love made you
Poor now.

FEAR

My siblings suffer from claustrophobia and agoraphobia. When attending church, they sit near an exit; when flying, they sit in a seat where they have the most room around them.

I understand that there are more than 300 phobias listed in medical books. These fears run the gamut from *pantophobia* (the fear of everything) to *futurphobia* (the fear of the future). Then we have *phobophobia* (the fear of being afraid).

If we are faith-walkers, we need not be afraid. Jesus says: "I am with you always." Here we have one of Jesus' wonderful promises! "Go, and I am with you every step of the way."

He is with us no matter how dark and gloomy it gets.

> "There is no fear in love, but perfect love casts out fear,
> for fear has to do with punishment,
> and whoever fears has not reached perfection in love.
> We love because he first loved us."[120]

What are your fears (out of the 300 or so)?
How do you rate your love?

---

[120] 1 John 4:18-19

CHRISTIANOPHOBIA

Just when we thought that we knew all the fears, now we have Christianophobia. It is a deadly fear for far too many who profess their faith in Christianity.

In too many places they are fair game for the extremists and for those who claim that they are protectors of their citizens.

Saint Pope John Paul II spoke about "the fear of Christianity" in a speech at Lourdes in 1983, although the word Christianophobia was coined by law professor and scholar Joseph H.H. Weiler and in use since 2004. The Catholic author and scholar George Weigel describes the phobia in detail in two of his books.

Mr. Weiler used the word Christianophobia to refer to the growing marginalization of Christians in Europe, but now the word has taken on a broader meaning: it refers to anti-Christian oppression and persecution wherever it takes place, and those places are on the increase as the daily media gives evidence.

In December 2004, Pope John Paul II argued that Christianophobia was on the rise throughout the world and he urged the United Nations to draft laws on it as it had done on Islamophobia and anti-Semitism. The late Pope Benedict XVI voiced his deep concern for Christianophobia and its snowballing in various countries. Since 1991, Iraq has lost two-thirds of its Christian population because of the deadly phobia.

The United Nations Human Rights Commission in Geneva now includes Christianophobia in its statements.

The House of Commons at Westminster Hall had a debate on Christianophobia in early December 2007 led by Mark Pritchard (The Wrekin) with Hywel Williams in the Chair. I found the debate very interesting.

Where do you stand on Christianophobia?

Indifferent, horrified, angry, moved to action?

WAITING

We wait. It is a necessary aspect of human life. We wait in the ER, in the dentist office, in line at the supermarket, in restaurants, at amusement parks, in the bank, to see a play, for the traffic light to change to green. We wait.

We wait for the baby to be born, to grow. We wait for our plants to grow, for our vegetables to ripen. We wait for our incisions to heal, for bread to rise, for cheese to age. We wait.

Carlo Carretto was Pope Pius XII's faithful leader of the Catholic Action Movement in Italy. At 44 years old, in 1954, Carlo heard the call of Jesus to join the Little Brothers of Jesus of Charles de Foucauld in Africa's Sahara.

Carretto has left us some insightful writings. They have deeply influenced the lives of thousands before and since his death in 1988 at 78 years old. In his book, *Letters from the Desert*, Carretto suggests those of us who live busy lives need to listen to God:

> "Be patient! Learn to wait for each other, for love, for happiness, for God."

We know the problem. We don't like to wait. We are impatient. We are "now" people. Now, we want everything, anything now. Fast is the magic word; now is the operative word.

In his book, *The God Who Comes*, Carretto wrote:

> "As we wait, we learn that we are not in control. Life in our middle years has a way of teaching us that, especially when we don't want to listen.
>
> "We must assume an attitude of waiting, accepting the fact that we are creatures and not creator. We must do this because it is not our right to do anything else...man is able to imitate nothing; he is able

only to accept. If God does not call, not calling takes place..."

So, we wait, and we pray. For to pray means to wait for the God who comes. Every prayer-filled day sees a meeting with him. Every night which we faithfully put at his disposal is filled with his presence.

PAULO COELHO

Do you know the Brazilian author Paulo Coelho? I discovered him while I was stationed in Kenya. His books convey a message and always turn up a few surprises. I recommend him.

Coelho tells a story about a time he was living in a hermitage in the Pyrenees. He came across a text engraved on a wall that he was convinced had been left there for him alone.

At the time, he was slightly upset at the lack of interest on the part of the editor of his book *The Alchemist* (which, incidentally, became a great success). Coelho kept repeating the text that he had found as a kind of mantra. Gradually, he obtained peace of mind.

This is the text – written by Carlo Carretto:

> "If you were really a child, a true child, instead of worrying about what you can't do, you would contemplate Creation in silence.
> And you would become used to looking calmly at the world, nature, history and the sky.
>
> If you really were a child, at this moment you would be singing Hallelujah for the things before you. Then – free from tensions, fears and useless questions – you would use this time to wait with curiosity and patience for the things in which you invested so much love to bear fruit."

May these words bring you peace of mind!

JESUS AT THE DOOR

William Holman Hunt has left us three versions of his famous painting of Jesus *The Light of the World*. Most of us probably have seen his life-sized version that hangs in Saint Paul's Cathedral, London, England. It is the version usually reproduced on holy cards and in printed materials.

Although the title of the painting comes from Jesus' words in Saint John 8:12, Hunt's idea stems from the Book of Revelation 3:20...

> "Listen! I am standing at the door and knocking; if you hear my voice and open the door, I will come into you and eat with you, and you with me."

There have been thought-provoking commentaries on the celebrated painting.

We see the crowned Jesus holding a lantern while he knocks at the door with no doorknob. It is dark, and we see bats in the distance.

The door is our human heart.

Only we can open the door because of the God-given free will.

What's inside?

Jesus with the crown of thorns reminds us of the gift of himself out of love on the cross.

The lantern with its decorations of stars and crescents show Jesus as King of the universe including Muslim countries.

An unknown fact: when Hunt finished the first version of the painting in 1853, he became a Christian.

I recommend getting a copy of *The Light of the World* for your personal reflection and meditation. It offers much fruit.

LOCKED DOORS

I recently stayed in the basement apartment of a priest residence in a major city. I was told that there was a ghost who sometimes made herself known. They suggested that I lock the door of my room at night.

I looked at them...Since when can locked doors stop ghosts?

During my five days in the basement, the ghost never appeared. The cook told me that she ordinarily stayed on his side of the floor. I think that this was supposed to relieve any anxiety on my part.

Remember the scene after the Resurrection? The apostles are in a locked room because of their fear of the Jewish authorities, and the Risen Jesus appeared. He was not stopped by any locked doors, and he appeared not as a ghost, but in his glorified body.

> "Jesus came and stood among them and said, 'Peace be with you'. After he said this, he showed them his hands and his side. Then the disciples rejoiced when they saw the Lord."[121]

Thomas was not there when Jesus appeared and did not believe the others about Jesus' appearance. Jesus made him wait eight days. Jesus tells Thomas, "Okay, here I am, touch my hands and side."

And we hear those words that millions have said ever since:

> "My Lord and my God."
> Jesus proclaims a beatitude:
> "Blessed are those who have not seen and yet have come to believe."[122]

That's us! How blessed are we!

---

[121] John 20:19-20
[122] John 20:29

SHEPHERDS

I conducted a Day of Prayer for the Society of Saint Vincent de Paul in Boise, Idaho. What a beautiful area! I could easily live there.

At my request, they took me to tour the Basque Museum which narrates the history of the Basque shepherds through that whole area of the United States. I used to hear the older priests in Colorado talk about these remarkable Basque shepherds. I was eager to see their museum.

I understand now that the Andeans have replaced the Basque because of a post 9/11 immigration policy. The current language is Quechua, the Andean language.

These shepherds, past and present, know loneliness, boredom, bad weather, and unpredictable danger. These men must watch what the animals eat, where they go, and protect them from mountain lions and wolf packs. The only ones the shepherds talk to are their Akbashes (dogs) who are fearless and will attack any predator.

In colder months, the shepherd lives in a *campito* (a trailer) that is moved from one spot to another across the valleys as needed.

Tradition tells us that an angel appeared to the shepherds first because they were poor and considered at the bottom of the social ladder. Perhaps, the angel knew that shepherds were known for their simplicity, courage, and tenacity, and yet they were frightened by the sudden appearance of the angel, but who wouldn't be?

> "In that region there were shepherds living in the fields, keeping watch over their flock by night. Then an angel of the Lord stood before them, and the glory of the Lord shone around them, and they were terrified. But the angel said to them, 'Do not be afraid; for see – I am bringing you good news of great joy for all the people: to you is born this day in the city of David a Savior, who is the Messiah, the Lord."[123]

---

[123] Luke 2:8-20

The one angel increases to a host of angelic voices.

Shepherds have plenty of private time, for prayer and reflection, praying for protection from sickness and injury, for assistance in caring for and saving their sheep.

What about you?

Do you have time to pray and to ponder?

Do you pray for yourself and for others?

APOPHATIC AND KATAPHATIC PRAYER

Wait a minute! I have enough trouble understanding meditation, contemplation, purgative, illuminative, and unitive, etc., now I am presented with apophatic and kataphatic prayer. What are we talking about? I never hear priests, deacons, or others using these words.

Let's look at some etymology.

Apophatic and kataphatic find their origin in Greek words.

Apophatic means negative. It is derived from a verb "to say no" or "to deny."

When I taught mysticism, I discussed the *via negativa* (the negative way).

Kataphatic means positive. It is derived from a verb "to say yes" or "to affirm."

Here we talk about *via positiva* (the positive way).

Apophatic prayer has no content. It means emptying our mind of words and ideas and simply resting in God's presence.

Kataphatic prayer has content. It uses words, ideas, images, and symbols.

The prayer that most of us use is kataphatic. Why? Because we use words, ideas, images, etc. We say our rosary, our novena, our favorite prayers, and we are using words and ideas.

But sometimes, we are graced with apophatic prayer.

We rest in the Lord and our mind is free from content. God's presence is enough!

How we enjoy this moment of grace!

CALUMNY, DETRACTION, LYING, RASH JUDGMENT

Are these recreational sports? Occupational diseases? Nothing to be concerned about, just part and parcel of life? No big deal, usually?

Remember the 8[124] Commandment? "You shall not bear false witness against your neighbor."[124]

How do people do that? How do we bear false witness against our neighbor? The bottom line: we misrepresent the truth in our relations with other people. This gets played out in distortion of the truth, or outright lying, or doing a number on someone (making up a story), or revealing some things we should not tell in the first place. Consider the tabloids and the media. Somebody is making a lot of money on "re-interpreting" or reinventing moral theology!

The tongue:

> "The tongue is a fire. The tongue is placed among our members as a world of iniquity; it stains the whole body, sets on fire the cycle of nature, and is itself set on fire by hell...no one can tame the tongue – a restless evil, full of deadly poison. With it we bless the Lord and Father, and with it we curse those who are made in the likeness of God. From the same mouth come blessing and cursing. My brothers and sisters, this ought not to be so."[125]

Respect for the reputation of others forbids...

- *rash judgment* – I assume something as true about my neighbor (a moral fault), but I really don't have sufficient knowledge.

---

[124] Exodus 20:16
[125] James 3:6-10

- *detraction* – I disclose my neighbor's faults and failings to another person who did not know them, and I do this without a valid reason
- *calumny* – I tell some things about my neighbor which are not true at all; I lie.
- *Lying* – I tell something false or untrue with the intention of deceiving my neighbor.

Character assassination is deadly. It is easier than we think: we can kill a person's good reputation – dishonor her or him.

We are dealing with justice here, not just charity.

GALILEE

A recent director of our community retreat reminded us that in the New Testament geography is more than geography. In Scripture, there are no "throw-away lines."

Places in Scripture are more than mere places: look for some deeper meaning.

How should we view Galilee for example? In Mark's Gospel, Jesus calls his first disciples by the Sea of Galilee. Here they learn to be Jesus' companions: to be with Jesus. Companion means with + bread.

Galilee is where Jesus established the first seminary. His chosen get their first assignments as disciples.

Galilee is a place of consolation and joy, a place of strength! It is a privileged place to meet the risen Jesus. It is a place of first love and zeal.

What is Galilee for you?

Does it have any significant meaning?

SILENCE

The BBC once ran a three-part series called *The Big Silence*. It was the series conducted then by Abbot Christopher Jamison of Worth Abbey in West Sussex, England.

The program involved three women and two men from high-pressured jobs in stressful lines of work. They were looking for something they sensed missing in their lifestyles and were looking for an opportunity to find a more spiritual dimension to their lives.

Abbot Christopher showed them the simple path to God: *Silence*.

From my personal experience, I find that people have a terrible time keeping silence during a day of prayer or retreat. This includes religious and priests…I'm talking everyone. It's mission impossible!

Our culture is a culture of doing, and when we are not doing, we feel uncomfortable. And we need noise. Our culture is a culture of noise.

Consider an intersection on a hot summer day. The car next to you is vibrating from the volume of the radio or streaming device – aided too by what is being played. And how many have a TV blasting morning, noon, and night? I know several people who have TV sets in every room of their apartment including the bathroom. And what about people on planes or walking down the streets listening to music? It is a *sine qua non* for many.

Our culture has a difficult time with silence.

But silence has many beneficial outcomes:

- stops us from distracting ourselves
- assists us in being reflective
- deepens us; we delve into greater truths more deeply
- provides us with ambiance to listen to God
- can help us to become aware of God's presence
- can help us feel God's love
- gives us a sacred place for our relationship: God and us

Silence is indeed golden – actually more precious than gold!

FRIENDSHIP

Friendship...

>   ...is basic to all human beings
>   ...we need stable friendships in our lives
>   ...our best friend accepts us for who we are; we can share
>   who we are with him/her...for example, with Jesus

Friendship

- dialogue
- confidential encounter
- presence
- intimacy
- spontaneity
- frequent and continual exchanges
- silence
- solitude
- exclusivity
- a loving response founded upon faith and trust
- fidelity
- mutuality

"If you are friends with Christ, many others will warm themselves at your fire...On that day when you no longer burn with love, many will die of the cold."[126]

"I have called you friends because I have made known to you everything that I have heard from my Father."[127]

"You are my friends if you do what I command you."[128]

"No one has greater love than this, to lay down one's life for one's friends."[129]

---

[126] Francois Mauriac
[127] John 15:15
[128] John 15:14
[129] John 15:13

24 HOURS IN THE LIFE OF JESUS

What was it like…what was 24 hours in the life of Jesus like?

Of course, every day had its differences as do our days, but Saint Mark gives us, in summary fashion, a good idea about a day in Jesus' public ministry.

It was a long day. It started before sunrise and ended far into the night. The day was centered primarily on others. Jesus is the "Man for Others," and we see this in how he spent most of the 24 hours as described in some detail by Saint Mark 1:21-39. The main activities of Jesus' ministry were preaching, teaching, and healing.

Jesus attended the synagogue at Capernaum, the center of his ministry, with his disciples. (He had just selected Simon Peter, Andrew, James, and John.) He teaches those in attendance and with a new authority unlike Rabbis and scribes.

He casts out an unclean spirit from a man on his own; usually a person asks for healing or a cure from Jesus; this was an unusual occurrence. Jesus took the initiative.

Jesus cures Simon's mother-in-law of a fever; she, in turn, waits on them, which I take as, provides them with a good meal.

In the evening, at sundown, they brought him others who were ill, and Jesus heals them.

In the early morning, while it is still dark, Jesus goes off to a deserted spot to pray. He must have had only a few hours of sleep.

In the course of time, Simon Peter tracks him down: "Everyone is looking for you."

Jesus immediately responds:

> "Let us go on to the neighboring towns, so that I may proclaim the message there also; for this is what I have come to do."[130]

And so Jesus begins a new 24 hours in his life.

Where does Jesus fit in your 24 hours?

---

[130] Mark 1:38

THE JESUS PRAYER

Father Tom Glynn is now deceased. He and I went back to high school days.

Tom was a priest of the Byzantine Rite, the Ukrainian Greek Catholic Church. He introduced me to Jesus' Beads and the Jesus Prayer at least fifty years ago. I believe that he was the one who gave me a copy of *The Way of the Pilgrim*. It is the story of a man whose goal was to discover how to pray without ceasing. I recommend that you read the book.

My Jesus Beads are a strand of 100 black woven beads – a devotional honoring the name of Jesus and imploring his mercy. It is called a *Chotki*. The strand may have 25 or 100 beads.

Jesus' Prayer is often referred to as The Prayer of the Heart.

The usual form of the Jesus' Prayer is: "Jesus, Son of God, have mercy on me, a sinner." The longer version is: "Jesus, Son of the Living God, have mercy on me, a sinner." This is the form I am accustomed to, although there are shorter ones also.

The fruit of the Jesus Prayer is that it becomes a prayer of the heart and an abiding presence of God. This presence is usually apophatic. What does that mean? It means that we pray without an image or concept; it just is, yet we experience God's presence in our heart.

The *Chotki* is traditionally used as a *breath prayer*, with "Lord Jesus Christ, Son of the Living God" prayed on inhaling, and "have mercy on me, a sinner" prayed on exhaling.

Over time, the Jesus Prayer prevents pride and feelings of dejection. It has been compared to a boat coming into the safe harbor, the harbor of humility.

"Jesus, Son of the Living God, have mercy on me, a sinner."

RELIGIOUS FREEDOM DAY

The United States has been celebrating Religious Freedom Day since 1786. We commemorate Virginia's 1786 Statute for Religious Freedom in which Thomas Jefferson wrote:

> "All men shall be free to profess, and by argument to maintain, their opinion in matters of religion."

The fundamental principle of religious freedom is enshrined in our country's Constitution's First Amendment.

The late Pope Benedict XVI issued a message 1 January 2011 on Peace, in which he reiterates, that religious freedom is the path to peace. The Archbishop of Leon, Mexico stated that without religious freedom it is impossible to create a just society.

The Holy Father and some civil leaders condemned the persecution and killings of persons because of their faith. Early in January every year, the Vatican releases the number of Catholic missionaries who have been murdered due to hatred of the faith or other reasons. The church avoids using the term "martyrs".

While the number of missionaries over the last several years has hovered between 20-40, the number of Christians has risen. More lay people are being killed by extremist groups and/or government forces.

My recommendation is that we pray for all those women and men who are hampered in the practice of their faith.

We thank God for the religious freedom that we enjoy in this beloved country!

JESUS IS CRAZY!

In his humanity, Jesus was vulnerable – open to suffering and even death.

He was called a variety of names, several not very flattering. I suspect that his chaste celibacy for a Jew 30 years old added to the litany of names. In Mark 3:20-21, we read:

> "Then he went home; and the crowd came together again, so that they could not even eat. When his family heard it, they went out to restrain him, for people were saying, 'He has gone out of his mind.'"

Some translations use the terms: "He was beside himself" or "he was crazy." This is quite an accusation: "Jesus was out of his mind."

Why did his extended family try to restrain his public ministry and keep him in Nazareth? I think that there are several reasons.

Here was a man who had lived a quiet, unassuming life as a trades-man for 30 years, and suddenly he leaves everything that offered security and serenity and goes through a water ceremony of a man named John the Baptist who, to many people, was out of his mind. Look at the way he dressed and what he ate and where he lived!

Here was a man who had a steady job and income, was a needed carpenter who did excellent work, and he leaves it all to be an itinerant preacher with no permanent residence or income. That is crazy!

Here was a man who gathered a small cohort of followers: fishermen who had absolutely no political savvy or social influence, a disliked tax-collector, a zealot engrossed in the opposition, and other questionable disciples. What was Jesus thinking?! That is crazy!

And, on top of this, he was including women in his entourage; this was taboo; against all tradition and customs.

Here was a man who began to turn the heat on; he was criticizing the power-brokers: The Pharisees and scribes; he called them hypocrites for one thing. Jesus' family was concerned because not only could he be arrested, but also they might be implicated and be persecuted for his inflammatory remarks. That is crazy – insane!

Here was a man who was calling God his Father and claiming that he was the Messiah What kind of talk is that? It is crazy!

Besides he was attracting large crowds, and this was making the Roman occupational forces nervous. That is crazy!

Here was a man who, suddenly, after 30 years, was performing unexplainable, incredible miracles. How do you explain this?

The family needed to stop Jesus and keep him at home – and to control him.

As a Christian, do people think that you are out of your mind?

JANUARY 22ND

On 22 January, Christians and non-Christians commemorate the anniversary of the United States Supreme Court decision of 22 January 1973, Roe vs. Wade. This decision has its roots in Dallas, Texas.

This horrific decision and its companion decision, Doe vs. Bolton, allowed abortion on demand through all nine months of pregnancy in all 50 states of the United States, for virtually any reason or no reason at all.

In 2001, the United States Conference of Catholic Bishops designated 22 January as a day of penance for violations to the dignity of the human person committed through acts of abortion, and of prayer for the full restoration of the legal guarantee of the right to life.

Why does the Catholic Church devote so much attention, time, and energy to abortion? There are other serious challenges to life today: end-of-life issues, euthanasia, capital punishment, HIV/AIDS, war, poverty, homelessness, embryonic stem cell research, and more.

Why the emphasis? Because abortion is the most serious challenge to the sacredness of human life – because unborn children are the most vulnerable members of society and most need of our protection. Unborn children are the innocent victims who must rely totally on others for care and protection – first on their mothers and then, on all of us.

Pope Benedict XVI prayed during a worldwide Vigil for All Nascent Human Life:

> "Reawaken in us respect for every unborn life,
> make us capable of seeing in the fruit of a mother's womb
> the miraculous work of the Creator,
> open our hearts to generously welcoming every child
> that comes into life."

Remember the infant Jesus: his Mother and foster-father were forced to flee to Egypt to prevent Herod from killing him as he was two years or under.[131]

---

[131] Matthew 2:16-23

Like pedophilia, abortion is a sin and a crime in the eyes of the church.

I invite you to join countless others in praying for the end of abortion in our world.

Roe v Wade was overturned by the US Supreme Court on June 24, 2022.

MIGRATION

Walking the streets of downtown Manhattan is always a wonder to me and an education. It is rare not to hear a "united nations" of voices: people talking on cell phones, or having lively conversations in various languages and dialects. Every block of downtown verifies that New York is a meeting pot of humanity. Standing on the corner waiting for the traffic light to change is a remarkable experience of people speaking in tongues!

Migration and immigration are getting to be dirty words in some countries of the world.

Every year, the church issues a message for the "World Day of Migrants and Refugees."

Many people must face the difficult experience of migration: internal or international, permanent or seasonal, economic or political, voluntary or forced. How often is migration due to fear of persecution? Often, migration is escape from tyranny.

For those people who have fled from violence and persecution, the international community has precise commitments: respect of their rights, legitimate concern for their security and social coherence, and a stable and harmonious coexistence to name a few significant guarantees according to the late Pope Benedict XVI.

Of course, countries have the right to regulate migration flows and to defend their own borders, always guaranteeing respect due to each human person. Immigrants have the duty to integrate into the host country and respect its laws and its national identity. It is a two-way street!

The practical words operative here are hospitality, solidarity, peace, safety, and unity.

Where do you stand with migrants and refugees?

It is always a hot topic!

WHATEVER HAPPENED TO....?

The Magi followed the star and venerated the newborn king, Jesus. They presented him through Mary and Joseph three gifts according to tradition: gold, frankincense, and myrrh. At first sight, these are three inappropriate gifts to give a newborn baby. Give baby clothes, diapers, blankets, toys, but those three gifts?!

We know the symbolism; authors have told us that gold is the gift for kings; frankincense is an ancient air purifier and perfume that was offered to God in Temple worship; and myrrh was an oriental remedy for intestinal worms in infants, used by the High Priest as anointing oil, and used in preparation of bodies for burial.

Whatever happened to those three gifts?

Did Joseph use the gold for traveling expenses? Did he buy carpentry tools with some of it? Perhaps Mary and Joseph bought themselves a small home.

Frankincense was worth a lot of money. Did they sell some of it for cash? Or did they keep it for domestic use?

Did Joseph and Mary give some of the myrrh away to a neighbor who had lost a loved for that person's burial? Or did they keep it for medicinal purposes?

What gifts would you have given the infant Jesus?

CHRISTMAS OR EASTER?

When I was a junior in high school several of us got into a friendly discussion: "Which is the greater feast, Christmas or Easter?" I took Christmas. Remember the bumper sticker: "Ask a teenager; they know everything."

Father Iggy Foley shot me down:

> "No, Easter, is the greater feast. The Son of God could have come into this world as an adult, not as an infant. After all, he is divine. All he had to do was give himself out of love for our sins in some form. He chose to be born out of love and to suffer and die on the cross out of love for our salvation."

Father Foley was right, Easter is the greater feast, but....

DO YOU SEE WHAT I SEE?

There is a difference between ocular vision and faith-vision.

The prophet Isaiah says:

> "He shall not judge by what his eyes see,
> or decide by what his ears hear.
> but with righteousness he shall judge the poor,
> and decide with equity for the meek of the earth.
> He shall strike the earth with the rod of his mouth,
> and with the breath of his lips he shall kill the wicked.
> Righteousness shall be the belt around his waist,
> and faithfulness the belt around his loins."[132]

Saint Vincent de Paul says:

> "I must not judge a poor peasant man or woman by their
> external appearance
> or their apparent intelligence, especially since very often
> they scarcely have the expression or the mind of rational
> persons, so crude and vulgar they are.
> But turn the medal, and you see by the light of faith that
> the Son of God, who willed to be poor, is presented to us
> by these poor people; that he scarcely had a human face
> in his passion, and passed for a madman in the mind of
> the Gentiles and a stumbling block in the mind of the
> Jews. With all that, he describes himself as the evange-
> lizer of the poor; *Evangelizare pauperibus misit me. O
> Dieu!* How beautiful it is to see people if we consider
> them in God and with the esteem in which Jesus Christ
> held them! If, however, we look on them according to

---

[132] Isaiah 11:3-5

the sentiments of the flesh and a worldly spirit, they will seem contemptible."[133]

When you look at the poor, what do you see?
Have you noticed a difference in your vision?

---

[133] CCD Vol. 11, #19, 26

CHRISTIAN IDENTIFICATION

There is one day of the year when people know if we are Catholics or Christians: Ash Wednesday.

They see us – and we see others – walking around with ashes on our foreheads.

I will never forget old Tom attending daily Mass in Chicago. I had just been ordained, and there was Tom with ashes on his forehead – in late June! I did a double take! (Tom was not an ordinary parishioner as I found out later in life when I became his pastor.)

But is there another way to identify Christians?

Is there something more reliable than ashes once a year?

We rely on Jesus.

He never said that people will know that we are Christians by the ashes on our foreheads. After all, they last for a day at most.

Jesus said:

"By this everyone will know that you are my disciples, if you have love for one another."[134]

---

[134] John 13:35

139

Many people reflect on Psalm 139 during retreats and days of recollection. Its twenty-four verses immediately make us pause for reflection.

> O Lord, you have searched me and know me.
> You know when I sit down and when I rise up;
> you discern my thoughts from far away.
> You search out my path and my lying down,
> and are acquainted with all my ways.
> Even before a word is on my tongue,
> O Lord, you know it completely.
> Such knowledge is too wonderful for me.
> it is so high that I cannot attain it. (vs.1-4, 6)

> Where can I go from your spirit?
> Or where can I flee from your presence?
> If I ascend to heaven, you are there.
> if I make my bed in She'ol, you are there. (vs.7-8)

> For it was you who formed my inward parts;
> you knit me together in my mother's womb.
> I praise you, for I am fearfully and wonderfully made.
> (vs.13-14)

> Search me, O God, and know my heart;
> test me and know my thoughts. (vs.23)

I recommend that you sit in silence and slowly reflect on any of these verses. You may want to read and pray the entire Psalm 139. It speaks to us about the basics of life and our essential relationship: God and ourselves.

THE DIVINE CAMPER

I am not a camper; thousands are; they love camping out in one of our National Parks or some location they particularly like. A priest friend of mine spends his vacation in Wyoming where he cannot be reached by phone and where he can rough it while he fishes.

In the prologue of Saint John's gospel, we read the main themes of the gospel: life, light, truth, the world, testimony, and the pre-existence of Jesus Christ, the Logos (the Word) who became man and who reveals God the Father. Read the prologue; it is truly like the overture of a musical or operetta which contains the major themes of what will appear later.

In John 1:14, we read:

> "And the Word became flesh and lived among us" – literally, in Greek, "and pitched his tent among us."

The Son of God – Jesus – came and pitched his tent among us; he is the divine camper!

He is still the divine camper in the tabernacles of the world. The word "tabernacle" comes from the Latin word that means "tent." Jesus' Real Presence is there in our tabernacles, our tents. He is present body, blood, soul, and divinity.

The Son of God pitched his tent and has never left us.

He is truly Emmanuel, "God with us."

POTENTIAL

I baptized my grandnephew, Julian Marten, in Milwaukee. It was a joyful celebration. One reason was a bunch of my grand-nieces and grand-nephews –from New York City to Phoenix and in-between were there. They were standing right near the font, various ages and sizes, their eyes glued on everything. I paused occasionally to explain the symbolism and the parts of the Sacrament of the Baptismal ceremony. I got several the kids nodding in agreement to my explanations: that it made sense to them (thank you, Lord!).

Julian Marten has great potential as does every child born. What will become of Julian Marten? Because of my age, I'm afraid that I will never know, but I pray that he will find true happiness and fulfillment in his life's vocation.

What he will become will depend on many circumstances: his parents, Sue and Kurt, educational opportunities, the rapidly changing American culture, the ups and downs of the political scene, and the list goes on. Ultimately, the potential depends on the "hand of the Lord."

"For, indeed, the hand of the Lord was with him."[135] These words were applied to the infant Jesus but can be applied to Julian Marten and to all the newly born.

The principal agent of growth is the Holy Spirit. We need to invoke the Spirit to enlighten us – to enkindle the fire of God's love within us – to empower us to uncover, to discover, the potential in each of us.

Come, Holy Spirit!

We need to invoke the Holy Spirit morning, noon, and night.

I pray for Julian Marten.

Pray for the infants you know and love.

---

[135] Luke 1:66

GOD IS A VERB

Many may not know the name, but our world owes much to Richard Buckminster Fuller. He has been hailed as an author, designer, an engineer, inventor, and futurist. His biography reads like an incredible movie script.

Although the geodesic dome had been created by Dr. Walter Bauersfeld, Fuller was awarded United States patents. He is credited for popularizing this structure. Geodesic domes have been used as civic buildings, exhibition attractions, part of military radar stations, to name the better-known usages. Perhaps you have seen one or more of his creations: The Spaceship Earth at Disney World's Epcot Center in Florida, The Gold Dome in Oklahoma City, the geodesic sphere in downtown Vancouver, British Columbia, Canada, the dome over a shopping center in downtown Ankara, Turkey, or the dome over a civic center in Stockholm, Sweden.

Fuller was an early environmental activist. He coined a principle he called *ephemeralization* meaning, in essence, "doing more with less."

In 1970, Fuller wrote *I Seem to Be a Verb*. He wrote:

> "I live on Earth at present, and I don't know what I am. I know that I am not a category. I am not a thing – a noun. I seem to be a verb...."

Fuller once said:
"God is a verb not a noun."

In one sense, Fuller's statement is not true! In another, it affirms something very important about our relationship with God. God is not, first, only a term from dogmatic theology or only a name from a creed and, in that sense, merely a proper noun. God is Father, Son, and Holy Spirit. God is living. Jesus, our risen Lord, is alive. The relationship between God and us is living and ongoing. *God is a verb!*

"God is love, and those who abide in love abide in God, and God abides in them."[136]

---

[136] 1 John 4:16

EXAMPLES FROM THE CROSS

We thank the great Dominican scholar, Saint Thomas Aquinas, for his insights. Thomas, remember, was born around 1225 and died 7 March 1274. I have had the privilege of praying at his burial site in Toulouse, France.

Saint Thomas asks the question: "Why did the Son of God have to suffer for us?" He gives a twofold answer: As a remedy for sin and as an example of how to act.

The passion of Christ completely suffices to fashion our lives. The cross exemplifies every virtue.

The example of love:

> No one has greater love than this, to lay down one's life for one's friends.[137]

The example of patience:

> He was oppressed, and he was afflicted, yet he did not open his mouth; like a lamb that is led to the slaughter, and like a sheep that before its shearers is silent. So he did not open his mouth.

> "Let us run with perseverance the race that is set before us, looking to Jesus, who for the sake of the joy that was set before him endured the cross, disregarding its shame..."[138]

The example of obedience:

> "For just by the one man's disobedience the many were made sinners, so by the one man's obedience the many will be made righteous."[139]

---

[137] John 15:13
[138] Hebrews 12:2
[139] Romans 5:19

The example of despising earthly things:

> He who is…the King of kings and Lord of lords. "It is he alone who has immortality and dwells in unapproachable light, whom no one has ever seen or can see…"[140]

Upon the cross he was stripped, mocked, spat upon, struck, crowned with thorns, and given only vinegar and gall to drink.

The example of detachment:

> "And when they crucified him, they divided his clothes among themselves by casting lots…"[141]

> Jesus was not attached to clothing, riches, honors, greatness, or anything delightful.

> "After twisting some thorns into a crown, they put it on his head."[142]

> And someone ran, filled a sponge with sour wine, put it on a stick, and gave it to him to drink…"[143]

What examples from the cross does Jesus give you?

---

[140] 1 Timothy 5:15-16
[141] Matthew 27:35
[142] Mathew 27:29
[143] Mark 15:36
(cf. Collatio 6 super Credo in Deum; while retaining the substance of the reading, this author has made alterations and identified the scripture quotes

RANDOM ACTS OF KINDNESS

The good thing about doing random acts of kindness is that anybody can do them, young or old…

- Mow the lawn for your neighbor who has a chronic illness
- Give a pregnant mother a seat on the crowded bus or subway
- Help someone carry their shopping bags to the car
- Clear off the windshield of the car for someone in a hurry on a cold morning
- Water the lawn while your neighbor is on vacation with their five kids
- Turn off your cell phone in church, at a meeting, in the doctor's office
- Shovel ice and snow off the sidewalk for your friend's mother
- Let someone get ahead of you in line at the supermarket checkout
- Rake the leaves for your neighbor who has returned from the hospital
- Open the door for someone walking in behind you
- Help someone up or down the escalator at the mall
- Invite someone out for lunch who has just lost their loved one
- Give someone a hand and run off pages on the copy machine for him/her
- Keep your eye on your neighbor's home while they are on vacation
- Babysit for a young couple's first baby so that they can have a night out
- Buy a breakfast or lunch or dinner secretly for a senior citizen living on social security

PS Add your own random acts of kindness to my list.

Little things mean a lot.
"By this everyone will know that you are my disciples, if you have love for one another."[144]

---

[144] John 13:35

"MAKE TIME TO LOVE THE EXCLUDED, DESPISED"

"Let us put into practice the call to do good to everyone, taking the time to love the least and most defenseless, the abandoned and despised, those who are discriminated against and marginalized."[145]

One of the subjects Pope Francis speaks so often about is those on the periphery of society. There are so many homeless, poor, and sick roaming our city streets – of large cities and small country cities as well.

The *Pro Petri Sede Association* was granted an audience with Pope Francis in February of 2023. During their audience, Pope Francis points out the generosity and solidarity of the early Christians as described in the Acts of the Apostles 4:32-35. Pope Francis said:

> "They were able to put everything in common to support their more fragile brothers and sisters."

> "They understood that they were the temporary stewards of their goods: indeed, all that we possess is a gift from God and we must let ourselves be enlightened by Him in the stewardship of the goods we receive."

He continued:

> "The Holy Spirit will always impel us to give to those in need, to fight poverty with what He gives us. For the Lord gives abundantly to us so that we in turn can give ourselves."

---

[145] Pope Francis, General Audience, 24 February 2023

IMPUTABILITY AND RESPONSIBILITY

The following is a quote from Pope Francis' Post-Synodal Apostolic Exhortation, *The Joy of the Gospel*.

> "Moreover, pastors and the lay faithful who accompany their brothers and sisters in faith or on a journey of openness to God must always remember what the *Catechism of the Catholic Church* teaches quite clearly:
>
> 'Imputability and responsibility for an action can be diminished or even nullified by ignorance, inadvertence, duress, fear, habit, inordinate attachments, and other psychological or social factors.' 'Consequently, without detracting from the evangelical ideal, they need to accompany with mercy and patience the eventual stages of personal growth as these progressively occur.'"[146]

I have used this quotation often in spiritual direction. I hope that you will find it as helpful if need be.

---

[146] The Joy of the Gospel, #44, Pope Francis, 24 November 2013

TWO

Martha and Mary. Two sisters – two sisters of Lazarus. Close friends of Jesus – where Jesus could go, have a nice meal, relax, and kick off his sandals.

Two attitudes – two attitudes that are important in the life of every Christian.

Two attitudes that are symbolic of two venues of attentiveness:

1. Attentive to the Word of God
2. Attentive to the needs of persons.

Two persons, two attitudes, two ways to be attentive:

> Mary at the feet of Jesus, listening, asking questions;
> Martha getting food ready in the kitchen for a good meal.

Two attitudes that demand total attention.

Mary and Martha – the two – symbolic of contemplative and active life. It is not a question of choice. We can't sacrifice one to retain the other. Both are necessary. One is not better than the other.

Both, the contemplative and the active, are service.

Saint Vincent de Paul calls his followers to be a Mary-Martha:

> Through the intimate union of prayer and apostolate the confrere becomes a contemplative in action and an apostle in prayer.[147]

I suggest a slow, reflective reading of Luke 10:38-42.

---

[147] Constitutions of the Congregation of the Mission, #42

SAINT PATRICK'S PRAYER

Many of us, whether of Irish descent or not, know something about Saint Patrick, but do we know the prayer that bears his name? It is a favorite of a good number of people.

> Christ be beside me.
> Christ be before me.
> Christ be behind me.
> King of my heart.
> Christ be within me.
> Christ be below me.
> Christ be above me.
> Never to part.
> Christ on my right hand.
> Christ on my left hand.
> Christ all around me.
> Shield in the strife.
> Christ in my sleeping.
> Christ in my sitting.
> Christ in my rising,
> Light of my life.

Obviously, there is more to Saint Patrick and his feast day of 17 March than green beer, corn beef and cabbage, and Irish soda bread.

Saint Patrick, pray for Ireland.

Pray for us all now and at the hour of our death. Amen.

PADRE PEDRO OPEKA, C.M.

I met the incredible Vincentian confrere only once if my memory is correct. I would very much like meeting with him again!

Padre Opeka was born in Argentina of Slovene parents, emigrants to South America to avoid the Yugoslavian Communist Regime. I believe that Pope Francis and he are good friends.

From the age of nine, Pedro learned bricklaying from his father.

As a young teen he had to choose: Become a professional soccer player or a priest. He chose priesthood in the Congregation of the Mission (the Vincentians).

In 1970, he went to Madagascar where he worked as a bricklayer in parishes conducted by the Vincentians.

Padre Opeka finished his studies at the Catholic Institute of Paris (1972-1975). He learned French there, one of the seven languages he speaks!

At the mission of Madagascar, Padre Pedro saw people rummaging through the garbage for food and sleeping in huts. I saw the same things in Nairobi, Kenya.

Padre Pedro founded *Akamasoa* (good friend) in 1989 as a movement to help the poorest of the poor on the site of the garbage dump. He has ministered there for fifty years.

Padre Opeka has furnished Akamasoa's residents with tools, opportunities and community to change their lives and families for the better.

He has received the Kiwanis International 2005 World Service Medal for his work among the poor. He has been nominated to the Raoul Wallenberg Prize of the Council of Europe. Saint Pope John Paul II visited Madagascar 29 April to 2 May, 1989. Pope Francis visited Akamasoa in 2019.

A LETTER TO VLADIMIR PUTIN: 2022

Padre Opeka has urged the president of Russia, Vladimir Putin, to immediately stop the war initiated against the Ukraine. In 2022 Padre Opeka wrote a letter to Putin in regards to this.

The letter comes from the heart of a true Vincentian missionary. It is written in strong, blunt language:

"Brother Vladimir Putin, the citizens of many countries feel great bitterness, sadness and shame for your actions which are expressions of madness and megalomania.

THE PLUS FACTOR

I came across this prayer some time ago...it says much! It is found in a book by Father Adonis Narcelles, Jr, SVD: *Poems, Prayers and Inspirations*.

I asked for HAPPINESS you gave me SADNESS instead
plus, a deep FAITH to live with my situation.

I asked for HEALTH you gave me SICKNESS instead
plus, the STRENGTH to accept my condition.

I asked for COMFORT you gave me IRRITATION instead
plus, the COURAGE to find meaning in it.

I asked for SUCCESS you gave me FAILURE instead
plus, the SATISFACTION in what I am and have.

I asked for VICTORY you gave me DEFEAT instead
plus, HUMILITY to learn from my mistakes.

I asked for BLESSINGS you gave me TRIALS instead
plus, PERSEVERANCE to search for your will.

I asked for ANSWERS but you only gave me QUESTIONS
plus, the adequate PEACE OF MIND.

THE DIATESSARON

God's word offers different facets
according to the capacity of the listener,
and the Lord has portrayed his message in many colors,
so that whoever gazes upon it can see in it what suits him.
Within it he has buried manifold treasures,
so that each of us might grow rich in seeking them out.

The word of God is a tree of life
that offers us blessed fruit from each of its branches.
So whenever anyone discovers some part of the treasure,
he should not think that he has exhausted God's word.
Instead he should feel that this is all that he was able to find
of the wealth contained in it.

Nor should he say that the word is weak and sterile
or look down on it simply
because this portion was all that he happened to find.
But precisely because he could not capture it all
he should give thanks for its riches.[148]

---

[148] A commentary on the Diatessaron by Saint Ephrem, deacon: 1, 18-10: SC 121, 52-53

COMMUNICATION?

Some years ago, Peter Shaffer's play *The Royal Hunt of the Sun* found its way to Broadway; I still find it intriguing. Critics talk about its theme: Francisco Pizzaro's expedition from Spain to Peru, an expedition in the name of gold and religion.

Toward the end of Act 1, the Dominican chaplain of the 170 Spaniards has a conversation with the King of the Incas who personally believes that he is a god. The Inca king-god challenges the Spaniards:

> "You kill my people; you make them slaves. By what power?
>
> And the Dominican says:
> 'By this.
> He offers a copy of a Bible to the king.
> The Word of God.'
>
> The king-god holds the Bible to his ear and listens intently. He shakes the book.
> No word!
>
> The king smells the book; he tries to taste it.
> He throws the bible down:
> God is angry with your insults."

As far as the Inca is concerned, communication is speaking, listening, and responding.

Perhaps what the Inca-king did with the Bible seemed weird or odd, but what do we read in the Book of Revelation?

> "Then the voice that I had heard from heaven spoke to
> me again, saying,
> 'Go, take the scroll that is open in the hand of the angel
> who is standing on the sea and on the land.

So I went to the angel and told him to give me the little scroll; and he said to me,

'Take it and eat; it will be bitter to your stomach, but sweet as honey in your mouth.'

So I took the little scroll from the hand of the angel and ate it;

it was sweet as honey in my mouth, but when I had eaten it, my stomach was made bitter."[149]

The message of the scroll is indeed sweet; it is Jesus himself, but the message becomes bitter in the stomach because of communicating the truth. The messengers may indeed suffer persecution or a worse fate!

---

[149] Revelations 10:8-10

ENEMIES

Newspapers from Baltimore to Los Angeles ran a sizable obituary on Bishop Samuel Ruiz Garcia, commonly called "Don Samuel". He died from complications from diabetes at 86 years old. The President of Mexico, Felipe Calderon, released a statement at his death, as did U.S. Secretary of State Hillary Clinton.

What was special about this tiny man from a "backwater" state in southern Mexico? He was bishop for 40 years of the Diocese of San Cristobal de las Casas and mediated a commission for the end of the turbulent problems between the government of Mexico and the indigenous Zapatista rebels.

Bishop Samuel learned four Mayan languages so that he could speak to the natives; he often rode a mule so that he'd be able to get into all areas of his diocese. He had attended the entire Vatican II Council as well as the second general conference of Medellin.

He was founder of the Fray Bartolome de las Casas Center for Human Rights in Chiapas. *Don Samuel* was the champion of the poor and indigenous of the area. As the American newspapers said, he became an icon of the struggle of the Mayan Indian groups who were so long maltreated and forced to work in slave-like conditions by rich landowners.

In an interview before his death, a religious sister asked him how he could live out Jesus' command to love one's enemies, when he had so many.

Bishop Samuel immediately replied:

"I have no enemies."

The interviewer shot back:

What do you mean you don't have enemies? They drove you here in an armored van, accompanied by armed bodyguards supplied by your own Mexican government.

"There are some who want to make themselves enemy to me, but I have no enemies."

What about you?
Can you say:

I have no enemies?

YOU AND I ARE AT WAR

Is it true: you and I are at war? YES! It's true.

"We are facing an enormous and dramatic clash between good and evil, death and life, the 'culture of death' and the 'culture of life.'[150]

"We find ourselves not only 'faced with' but necessarily 'in the midst of' this conflict."[151]

I remember a Native American story that illustrates this reality so well...

> "Inside each of us live two wolves – a good wolf and a bad wolf.
> The good wolf tells us to obey our parents, be kind to old or sick people
> and choose friends who will do the same. But the bad wolf tells us
> it is more fun to disobey and do mean things to people.
> You have to decide which wolf to feed." *(Source unknown)*

The reality -- the challenge – the decision.

> *The reality is*: I do experience an inner warfare: the good wolf vs. the bad wolf.

> *The challenge*: To deal with this daily.

> *The decision*: I myself must decide multiple times of my waking hours which wolf to feed? The feedings are indeed constant.

I also must be aware of the external warfare in life: the "culture of death" vs "the culture of life."

We are warriors!

---

[150] Evangeliam Vitae, #28, Pope John Paul II, 25 March 1995
[151] Ibid.

LOVE – LIFE – LOVE

Is it true: A life without love is no life at all"?
Remember the song? Dean Martin sang it, as has Michael Bublé...

"You're nobody until somebody loves you."[152]

Saint Pope John Paul II wrote:

"Man cannot live without love.
He remains a being that is incomprehensible for himself,
his life is senseless, if love is not revealed to him,
if he does not encounter love, if he does not experience it
and make it his own, if he does not participate intimately
in it."[153]

The Danish philosopher Soren Kierkegaard has given us much food
for thought. Here are two examples.

- "Life can only be understood backwards, but it must be lived
  forward.

Life is not a problem to be solved, but a reality to be experienced."

- "God loves you where you're at, but he loves you so much that he
  doesn't want you to stay there."

I don't know where I read this:

"Let doctors handle your body,
God handle your life,
But you be in charge of your own moods."

Life, love, life. A few good quotes for prayerful reflection.

---

[152] Morgan, Stock, & Cavanaugh
[153] Redemptor Hominis, #10.1, 4 March 1979

LADIES IN WHITE

Every Sunday the Ladies in White attend mass at La Iglesia de Santa Rita in Havana, Cuba near Parque Miramar. After mass, they silently walk down 5th Avenue past international embassies protesting the imprisonment of their husbands and loved ones. The color white symbolizes peace.

During the Black Spring of 2003, the month of March, the Cuban government arrested and summarily tried and sentenced seventy-five individuals for a variety of reasons. These men were human rights defenders, independent journalists, and independent librarians; their terms ranged up to twenty-eight years.

Each Lady in White wears a button with a photo of her jailed relative and the number of years to which he has been sentenced.

As you can imagine, the Ladies in White have not had an easy time of it. They have suffered various attacks from the state security forces and counter-protesters. Cardinal Jaime Ortega, Archbishop of Havana, has intervened; Fifty-two political prisoners were released and the Ladies in White received permission to walk without incident.

The Ladies in White received the Sakharov Prize for Freedom of Thought in 2005, but the Cuban government refused permission for any of the group's leaders to attend the award ceremony in Strasbourg, France.

> "A prison cell, in which one waits, hopes…and is completely dependent on the fact that the door of freedom has to be opened from the outside…"[154]

> "True peace is born of doing the will of God, and bearing with patience the sufferings of this life, and does not come from following one's own whim or selfish desire,

---

[154] Dietrich Bonhoeffer

for this always brings, not peace and serenity, but disor-
der and discontent.[155]

"Peace I leave with you; my peace I give to you. I do not
give to you as the world gives. Do not let your hearts be
troubled, and do not let them be afraid."[156]

---

[155] Blessed Pope John XIII
[156] John 14:27

CONFESSIONS

One of the greatest things I have enjoyed throughout my priesthood is hearing confessions.

I, as a priest, do not forgive the sins of someone, Jesus does. Jesus uses me as his instrument, his agent.

As a sinner, myself, I have known how difficult it is, at times, to confess my sins, even to Jesus. We human beings are so weak, so capable of any offense against God's commandments. We feel ashamed.

Pope Francis reminds us priests:

> "I want to remind priests that the confessional must not be a torture chamber but rather an encounter with the Lord's mercy which spurs us on to do our best. A small step, in the midst of great human limitations, can be more pleasing to God than a life which appears outwardly in order but moves through the day without confronting great difficulties. Everyone needs to be touched by the comfort and attraction of God's saving love, which is mysteriously at work in each person, above and beyond their faults and failings."[157]

---

[157] The Joy of the Gospel, #44, Pope Francis, 24 November 2013

JESUS

All Christian spirituality should begin and end with Jesus. Although I wrote about him earlier in the manuscript, I end it with Jesus.

Saint Luke tells us in the Book of Acts:

> "And there is salvation in no one else, for there is no other name under heaven given among men by which we must be saved."[158]

Saint Paul reminds us:

> "At the name of Jesus every knee should bow, in heaven and on earth and under the earth, and every tongue confess that Jesus Christ is Lord, to the glory of God the Father"[159]

Jesus is worshipped in heaven:

> "And they sang a new song, saying, 'Worthy are you to take the scroll and to open its seals...from every tribe and tongue and people and nation...'"[160]

Jesus is venerated even in hell, because that sacred name is the terror of Satan and his demons.

> "In my name, they will cast out demons."[161]

Jesus is worshipped on earth by you and me.
Our reasons? Review the above quotes.
Thank you.

---

[158] Acts 4:12
[159] Philippians 2:10
[160] Revelations 5:9
[161] Mark 16:17

ACKNOWLEDGEMENTS

All Scripture quotes taken from Catholic Revised Standard Edition.

I have striven to acknowledge all the quotes from the multiple examples I have cited.

If I have omitted anyone or anything, I am truly sorry and will correct it in the next printing.

In my long life, I have read much. Unfortunately, I cannot recall the exact references. I wish I could.

IN APPRECIATION

I am very grateful to my dear friend Cardinal Timothy Michael Dolan for writing the preface for this book. Our friendship goes back many years!

I would like to thank Mrs. Mary Hoehn for the right to the photos shot of the author in the Mary, Mother of God Chapel. I am grateful to Mary for all the assistance she gave me in getting this book ready for publication.

Printed in the United States
by Baker & Taylor Publisher Services